# NTC's DICTIONARY OF THE
# United States

# NTC's Dictionary of the United States

*A Practical Guide to American Language and Culture*

George Kurian

*NTC Publishing Group*

Library of Congress Cataloging-in-Publication Data

Kurian, George Thomas.
　　NTC's dictionary of the United States : a practical guide to American language and culture / George Kurian.
　　　p.　cm.
　　ISBN 0-8442-5862-8 (cloth)
　　ISBN 0-8442-5863-6 (paper)
　　　1. United States—Civilization—1970-　—Dictionaries.　2. Popular culture—United States—Dictionaries.　I. Title.
　　E169.12.K863　1998
　　973.92'03—dc21　　　　　　　　　　　　　　　　　　　　　97-24618
　　　　　　　　　　　　　　　　　　　　　　　　　　　　　　　　CIP

Originally published as *NTC's Dictionary of the USA*

Cover design by Jeanette Wojtyla
Cover illustration copyright © by Phil Scheuer
Interior design by Mary Lockwood


Published by NTC Publishing Group
A division of NTC/Contemporary Publishing Group, Inc.
4255 West Touhy Avenue, Lincolnwood (Chicago), Illinois 60646-1975 U.S.A.
Copyright © 1998 by NTC/Contemporary Publishing Group, Inc.
All rights reserved. No part of this book may be reproduced, stored in a retrieval system, or transmitted in any form or by any means, electronic, mechanical, photocopying, recording, or otherwise, without the prior permission of NTC/Contemporary Publishing Group, Inc.
Printed in the United States of America
International Standard Book Number: 0-8442-5862-8 (cloth)
　　　　　　　　　　　　　　　　　　　0-8442-5863-6 (paper)
18　17　16　15　14　13　12　11　10　9　8　7　6　5　4　3　2　1

# Contents

| | |
|---|---|
| Photograph Credits | VII |
| Introduction | IX |
| How to Use This Dictionary | XI |
| Dictionary of the United States | 1 |

# Photograph Credits

All photographs are courtesy Archive Photos, with the following exceptions:

page 5, courtesy Archive Photos/Consolidated News

pages 17, 51, 115, 120, 129, 149, and 225, courtesy Archive Photos/Lambert

pages 23, 47, 167, and 181, courtesy Archive Photos/American Stock

page 60, courtesy Archive Photos/J. Sommer Collection

page 64, courtesy Archive Photos/Express Newspapers

page 91, courtesy Archive Photos/Nordisk Pressefoto

page 119, courtesy Archive Photos/Russell Reif

page 138, courtesy Archive Photos/Reuters/Drew

page 213, courtesy Archive Photos/Russell Thompson.

# Introduction

Much has happened in the New World since the settlement of the Jamestown colony in Virginia in 1607. In almost 400 years, its population has grown to more than a quarter of a billion people, and many facets of American life—from the *hamburger* to *jazz*—have become part of worldwide culture.

Thousands of books have been written about the United States of America, and it would be folly to suggest that this small volume embraces all that has been written before. It does, however, list the highlights of U.S. history and culture.

The following pages present a good sampling of the famous and significant people, places, things, and ideas that signify the USA. The reader will find entries describing the people who made the country great as well as those remembered primarily for their villainy; musical forms ranging from *ragtime* to *rap*; important holidays; national parks; food; political and social movements; historical events; and more. Photographs showing some of the faces and places of the USA complement the text.

Anyone eager to learn about the USA—visitors, recent immigrants, students of American language and culture—will enjoy browsing through these informative pages.

# How to Use This Dictionary

Using this dictionary is easy. The entries are alphabetized, ignoring spaces and punctuation. Each entry head is **boldfaced** at the beginning of the entry. When an entry is mentioned within a definition of another entry, it appears in SMALL CAPITALS. These cross-references help lead the browser onward to related entries.

Names are listed as entries in the dictionary last name first (for example, **Lincoln, Abraham**). When a name is cited within an entry, however, it appears first name first, as it would in a sentence (for example, ABRAHAM LINCOLN). The person's year of birth and year of death follow. When the exact year of birth has not been established, the approximate year of birth is given, preceded by "c," as in c1657.

Many abbreviations are listed, with a cross-reference to the spelled-out entry. This enables the reader to easily find the full names for familiar acronyms.

# NTC's Dictionary of the
# United States

**A.A.** Associate in Arts.

**AA** Alcoholics Anonymous.

**AAA** American Automobile Association. Pronounced "Triple A."

**AARP** American Association of Retired Persons.

**ABA** American Bar Association.

**Abbott, George** 1887–1994. Theatrical producer. A playwright and producer among whose successful plays were *Pal Joey*, *A Tree Grows in Brooklyn*, and *A Funny Thing Happened on the Way to the Forum*.

**ABC** American Broadcasting Companies, one of the three major television networks in the United States, along with CBS and NBC. In addition to television stations, ABC owns radio stations and some publications. All three networks suffered losses of viewers with the advent of cable television, videocassette rentals, and new networks in the 1980s and 1990s.

**Abernathy, Ralph David** 1926–1990. Civil rights leader. A close associate of MARTIN LUTHER KING, JR., Abernathy became the leader of the Southern Christian Leadership Conference after King's death.

**Abilene** a KANSAS railhead which, as the northern terminus of the CHISHOLM TRAIL, was a Wild West cow town in the 19th century.

**abolitionist** before the CIVIL WAR, a person who favored the abolition of slavery in the United States.

**Academy Awards** awards presented annually by the Academy of Motion Picture Arts and Sciences for excellence in film acting, direction, and production. The award itself, called an *Oscar* since 1931, is a gold statuette of a knight standing on a roll of film. (Also called the *Oscars*.)

**acid rock** rock music with a repetitive beat and lyrics evoking psychedelic experiences.

**ACLU** AMERICAN CIVIL LIBERTIES UNION.

***Acres of Diamonds*** an inspirational book by Russell H. Conwell (1843–1925), a Baptist minister, published in 1888. Conwell delivered thousands of lectures based on his book.

*the Oscar, the statuette presented to winners at the Academy Awards*

**ACT** AMERICAN COLLEGE TEST.

**ACT-UP** AIDS COALITION TO UNLEASH POWER.

**Acuff, Roy** 1903–1992. Singer. Called the King of Country Music, he was the first major star of the GRAND OLE OPRY.

**Adams, Ansel** 1902–1984. Photographer. Adams was known for his high-contrast, black-and-white scenes of the American West, which helped to popularize the national parks.

**Adams, Henry Brooks** 1838–1918. Historian and biographer. Son of one of the most prominent NEW ENGLAND families, Adams is noted for two classic works, *Mont-Saint Michel and Chartres* (1904) and *The Education of Henry Adams* (1906).

**Adams, John** 1735–1826. Second president of the United States (1797–1801). He was also the first vice president, from 1789 to 1797.

**Adams, John Quincy** 1767–1848. Sixth president of the United States (1825–1829).

**Addams, Jane** 1860–1935. Peace activist, social worker, reformer, and winner of the Nobel Peace Prize in 1931. Her most lasting work was the establishment of the Hull House in Chicago, ILLINOIS (1889).

**Adelphean** the first sorority, established in 1851 in Georgia's Wesleyan College.

**Adirondack Mountains** a mountain range in northeast NEW YORK. The highest point is Mount Marcy (5,344 ft).

**adjustable rate mortgage** a mortgage interest rate that can be changed upward or downward at regular intervals during the course of the loan term. Abbreviated ARM.

**adjusted gross income** a taxpayer's total income less adjustments to income, such as IRA deductions, alimony payments, Keogh retirement plan deductions, etc. Abbreviated AGI.

**adobe** 1. a type of brick made of sun-dried clay or earth. 2. a building made of such bricks, popular in the Southwest. First built by NATIVE AMERICANS, adobes are cool in the summer, warm in the winter, and fireproof.

**ADR** AMERICAN DEPOSITARY RECEIPT.

**aerobics** a physical fitness program that correlates oxygen consumption and pulse rate with various exercises.

*adobes*

**AFC** AMERICAN FOOTBALL CONFERENCE.

**AFDC** AID TO FAMILIES WITH DEPENDENT CHILDREN.

**affinity group** an organized group of people with similar professional or social interests.

**affirmative action** legislatively sanctioned efforts to improve the educational and employment opportunities of certain minorities and women.

**affluent society** a society characterized by economic prosperity and an abundance of consumer goods. From *The Affluent Society*, a book by economist JOHN KENNETH GALBRAITH, published in 1958.

**AFL** AMERICAN FEDERATION OF LABOR.

**AFL-CIO** American Federation of Labor and Congress of Industrial Organizations. A federation of over 100 trade and industrial unions that assists unions in organizing and promotes the activities of union members. The AFL and the CIO merged in 1955.

**African-American** 1. since the 1980s, the preferred name for a black American, formerly called a NEGRO. 2. of or pertaining to Americans of African descent.

**afro** a bouffant hairstyle popular among AFRICAN-AMERICAN men and women in the 1970s. It gave the appearance of a luxuriant growth of hair.

**AFT** AMERICAN FEDERATION OF TEACHERS.

**AFTRA** AMERICAN FEDERATION OF TELEVISION AND RADIO ARTISTS.

**Agassiz, Jean Louis Rodolphe** 1807–1873. Educator and naturalist. He was the founder of the Harvard Museum of Comparative Zoology.

**AGI** ADJUSTED GROSS INCOME.

**aha reaction** a sudden breakthrough or insight, as the culmination of a creative thinking process.

**Ahab, Captain** the hero of HERMAN MELVILLE's novel *Moby Dick* whose maniacal pursuit of the white whale leads to his tragic death.

**Aid to Families with Dependent Children** a government aid program within the DEPARTMENT OF HEALTH AND HUMAN SERVICES. Individual states determine eligibility and the benefits received. Abbreviated AFDC.

**AIDS Coalition to Unleash Power** an activist organization committed to direct action to end the AIDS crisis. Abbreviated ACT-UP.

**Ailey, Alvin** 1931–1989. Choreographer and dancer. He was the founder of the Alvin Ailey American Dance Center, known for its vivid portrayals of black experience through dance.

**Air Force One** the plane in which the president of the United States travels.

**AK** ALASKA. (The official two-letter post office abbreviation.)

**AL** 1. ALABAMA. (The official two-letter post office abbreviation.) 2. AMERICAN LEAGUE.

*Air Force One*

**Alabama** a state in the southeastern United States. Its capital is Montgomery and its largest city is Birmingham. Called the Yellowhammer State, Alabama's state bird is the yellowhammer and its state flower is the camellia. Abbreviated AL.

**Alamo** a Spanish mission in San Antonio, TEXAS, the site of a famous battle in the Texas War for Independence, in which nearly 200 Americans lost their lives on March 6, 1836.

**Alaska** the largest state in the United States, it borders the Arctic Ocean, Canada, the Pacific Ocean, and the Bering Sea. Its capital is Juneau and its largest city is Anchorage. Called the Land of the Midnight Sun or The Last Frontier, Alaska's state bird is the willow ptarmigan and its state flower is the forget-me-not. Abbreviated AK.

**Albee, Edward** 1928–. Playwright. Albee's early plays were characteristic of the theater of the absurd. Among his works are *Who's Afraid of Virginia Woolf?* (1962) and *A Delicate Balance* (1966).

**Alcatraz** federal prison from 1933 to 1963, nicknamed the Rock, on the rocky Alcatraz Island in San Francisco Bay. Originally a Spanish fortress, it was considered escape-proof.

**Alcoholics Anonymous** an organization founded in 1935 whose members help each other achieve and maintain sobriety. Members work through twelve steps that help them manage their lives. Abbreviated AA.

**Alcott, Amos Bronson** 1799–1888. Transcendentalist, father of LOUISA MAY ALCOTT. A pioneer of child-centered education, Alcott anticipated many of the educational theories of JOHN DEWEY. He was founder of the Temple School and the utopian community of Fruitlands.

**Alcott, Louisa May** 1832–1888. Novelist. Alcott is known for her domestic novels, especially *Little Women*, which drew on her own family life. Daughter of social reformer AMOS BRONSON ALCOTT, she was also a leader of the women's suffrage and temperance movements.

**Alger, Horatio** 1. 1834–1899. Author. Alger, a Unitarian minister, wrote over 100 rags-to-riches tales that extolled the self-made person. 2. a self-made person.

**Algonquian** a large family of languages that includes those spoken by many different NATIVE AMERICAN tribes.

**Algonquin** 1. a group of NATIVE AMERICAN tribes that inhabited the area between the St. Lawrence River and VIRGINIA, including the Narragansett, Mohican, DELAWARE, Shawnee, and Powhatan peoples. 2. the language spoken by the Algonquin.

**Algonquin Round Table** a group of writers who met informally between 1920 and 1940 in the dining room of New York City's Algonquin Hotel. The most prominent members of the group were DOROTHY PARKER, ALEXANDER WOOLLCOTT, and GEORGE S. KAUFMAN.

**Ali, Muhammad** 1942–. Boxer, born Cassius Clay. Heavyweight champion from 1964 to 1967 and from 1974 to 1978, Ali is considered one of the greatest boxers of all time. His flamboyant personality and unique boxing style made him famous worldwide.

**all-American** designating a select group, especially of athletes, considered as most representative or as the best.

**Allegheny Mountains** a mountain range in the APPALACHIAN MOUNTAINS in PENNSYLVANIA, MARYLAND, VIRGINIA, and WEST VIRGINIA varying in height from 2,000 to 4,000 ft.

**Allen, Ethan** 1738–1789. REVOLUTIONARY WAR hero. He led the Green Mountain Boys in their capture of Fort Ticonderoga from the British in 1775 and championed the independence of VERMONT.

**Allen, Fred** 1894–1956. Comedian and radio show host. Born John F. Sullivan, his *Fred Allen Show* ran from 1939 to 1949.

**Allen, Woody** 1935–. Filmmaker, actor, and comedian. Born Allen Konigsberg. His movie *Annie Hall* won an ACADEMY AWARD in 1977.

**aloha shirt** a light-colored, brightly patterned sports shirt.

**Aloha State** HAWAII. From *aloha*, Hawaiian for "love."

**alphabet agency** any of various government agencies better known by its initials, such as the FBI or FCC.

**alternative rock** a form of rock music that blends HEAVY METAL and mainstream pop.

**AMA** AMERICAN MEDICAL ASSOCIATION.

**ambulance chaser** a personal injury attorney who encourages accident victims to become his clients and sue for damages.

**America** a popular term for the United States, but strictly applicable to the two continents of the Western Hemisphere. From Amerigo Vespucci, Florentine navigator who first called the NEW WORLD a continent.

**"America the Beautiful"** the unofficial national anthem of the United States based on an 1893 poem by Katherine Lee Bates set to music by Samuel A. Ward. It celebrates the natural beauty of the land from "sea to shining sea."

**American Association of Retired Persons** a nonprofit organization open to anyone fifty years of age or older. It addresses the needs of older people and promotes independence and dignity. Abbreviated AARP.

**American Automobile Association** a travel organization whose services include planning trips and vacations, placing hotel and transportation reservations, and providing insurance and road service. Also called AAA, or Triple A.

**American Bar Association** founded in 1878, an organization of lawyers, judges, law students, and teachers pledged to uphold legal education and ethics. The ABA determines accreditation for law schools.

**American Civil Liberties Union** an organization that defends constitutionally protected rights and freedoms. Abbreviated ACLU.

**American College Test** a standardized exam required by several colleges for admission. It tests academic aptitude in English, mathematics, social studies, and natural sciences. Abbreviated ACT.

**American depositary receipt** a security issued in the United States representing a security issued in a foreign country. ADRs can be bought and sold in the United States just like the underlying shares. Abbreviated ADR.

**American dream** material and social success, believed to be the reward for hard work in America, the land of opportunity.

**American Federation of Labor** a powerful labor organization that merged with the CIO in 1955. Abbreviated AFL. See AFL-CIO.

**American Federation of Teachers** founded in 1916, an organization of education workers that promotes professionalism, wages, and job security and addresses classroom issues such as class size and equal opportunity. Abbreviated AFT.

**American Federation of Television and Radio Artists** the labor union for people working in live and videotaped television programming, commercials, and radio broadcasting. Abbreviated AFTRA.

**American Football Conference** one of the two divisions of the NATIONAL FOOTBALL LEAGUE. Abbreviated AFC.

*American Gothic* a starkly realistic 1930 portrait of a midwestern farm couple created by painter Grant Wood (1892–1942).

*American Language, The* See MENCKEN, H. L.

**American League** one of the two professional baseball leagues in the United States. The other is the NATIONAL LEAGUE. Each league is further broken down into three divisions, Central, East, and West. At the end of the baseball season, the first-place teams from each division (the winners of the PENNANT) play each other, and the winner goes on to the WORLD SERIES. Abbreviated AL.

**American Legion** a veterans' organization founded in 1919 that promotes conservative and patriotic ideals and military preparedness.

**American Medical Association** founded in 1847, an organization of doctors that promotes health and wellness. Abbreviated AMA.

*American Mercury, The* See NATHAN, GEORGE JEAN.

**American Red Cross** the American branch of the Red Cross, an international organization that administers health programs and provides relief to victims of war and natural disasters. Abbreviated ARC.

**American Revolution** See REVOLUTIONARY WAR.

**American Samoa, Territory of** a U.S. territory located in the South Pacific Ocean, composed of five islands and two atolls. Abbreviated AS.

**American Sign Language** a language used by deaf and hearing-impaired people in the United States. It uses hand signs and gestures. Abbreviated ASL or Ameslan.

**American Sphinx** ULYSSES S. GRANT.

**American Standard Code for Information Interchange** a way of storing letters and numbers in a computer file so that many different programs can read them. Abbreviated ASCII.

**American Stock Exchange** a stock market for small investors and organizations that do not meet the size requirements of the New York Stock Exchange. Abbreviated ASE or Amex.

**Americana** material relating to or printed in America or written by Americans. Properly restricted to the period before 1820.

**America's Cup** a famous international yacht race and the large silver cup that is presented as a trophy to the winner of the race. The trophy was in American hands from 1851 to 1983.

**Ameslan** AMERICAN SIGN LANGUAGE.

**Amex** AMERICAN STOCK EXCHANGE.

**Amish** a Mennonite sect, also known as the Old Order Mennonites, followers of the 17th-century Swiss reformer, Jacob Amman. They immigrated to the United States from Germany in the 18th century and settled in Lancaster County, PENNSYLVANIA. Known as Plain People for their simple lifestyles, they reject commercial products, such as store-bought clothing, automobiles, and electricity.

**Amtrak** the National Railroad Passenger Corporation, an organization of railroad companies in the United States.

**anchor** a newscaster who coordinates a radio or television program. Also *anchorman, anchorwoman*.

**"Anchors Aweigh"** the official service song of the U.S. Navy, composed in 1908 by Charles Zimmerman and Alfred Miles.

**Anderson, Marian** 1902–1993. Opera singer. The first African-American star at the METROPOLITAN OPERA, she was celebrated for the range of her voice, described as "heard once in a hundred years."

**Anderson, Sherwood** 1876–1941. Novelist. He is best known for his short-story collection, *Winesburg, Ohio* (1919).

**anglo** a Mexican term for white Anglo-Saxons.

*Marian Anderson*

**Annapolis** the site of the U.S. Naval Academy, founded in 1845. Also, the capital of MARYLAND.

**answering machine** a tape recorder that responds to a telephone call with a recorded message and records incoming messages from callers.

**antebellum** of or relating to the period before the CIVIL WAR.

**Anthony, Susan B.** 1820–1906. Women's suffrage leader. Known as the Napoleon of the women's rights movement, Anthony was a spirited Quaker and temperance activist whose crusades helped to pass the Nineteenth Amendment, granting women the right to vote.

**anticipointment** a disappointment that is directly proportional to the level of anticipation generated by unrealistic promises.

**antitrust** relating to a legislative enactment or executive department order designed to promote free market competition and reduce or eliminate monopolistic cartels.

**A & P** Trademark. Great Atlantic and Pacific Tea Company, a United States supermarket chain.

**AP** ASSOCIATED PRESS.

**Apache** NATIVE AMERICAN people of the Southwest who gained a reputation as fierce warriors in the 19th century.

**APB** all points bulletin; a bulletin transmitted to law-enforcement agencies, usually to describe a wanted person or persons.

**APO** Army Post Office. A post office on an army base.

**Appalachia** the economically backward uplands of KENTUCKY and VIRGINIA.

**Appalachian Mountains** a mountain range in the eastern United States that extends from Quebec, Canada, to the Gulf of Mexico.

**Appaloosa** a white or light gray horse dappled with brown markings, originally bred by Nez Percé Indians.

*Appaloosa*

**apple pandowdy** a deep-dish, sweet pie made with apples and molasses.

**Appleseed, Johnny** 1775–1845. Itinerant preacher, born John Chapman. Appleseed spent 40 years crisscrossing the OHIO wilderness, wearing a coffee-colored sack tunic and a tin hat and planting appleseeds wherever he went.

**Appomattox Court House** a small town in VIRGINIA where on April 9, 1865, ROBERT E. LEE surrendered the Army of Northern Virginia to ULYSSES S. GRANT, marking the end of the CIVIL WAR.

**AR** ARKANSAS. (The official two-letter post office abbreviation.)

**Arbor Day** a day set apart in many states for planting trees.

**ARC** AMERICAN RED CROSS.

**area code** a three-number code that precedes a telephone number. It identifies the general location of the person being called.

**Arendt, Hannah** 1906–1975. Political philosopher. German-born Arendt was a lifelong opponent of totalitarianism. The best known of her works is *The Human Condition* (1958).

**Arizona** a state in the southwestern United States. Called the Grand Canyon State, its capital and largest city is Phoenix. Arizona's state bird is the cactus wren and its state flower is the flower of the SAGUARO CACTUS. Abbreviated AZ.

**Arkansas** a state in the southern United States. Called the Land of Opportunity, its capital and largest city is Little Rock. Arkansas' state flower is the apple blossom, and its state bird is the mockingbird. Abbreviated AR.

**Arlington National Cemetery** a 500-acre cemetery established in 1864 in Arlington, VIRGINIA, as the burial place for Americans killed in the service of their country. It contains the TOMB OF THE UNKNOWN SOLDIER and the memorial to President JOHN FITZGERALD KENNEDY.

**ARM** ADJUSTABLE RATE MORTGAGE.

**Armistice Day** former name for VETERANS DAY.

**Armory Show** an exhibition of paintings held at the 69th Regiment Armory in New York City in 1913. The exhibition made history by displaying for the first time in the United States many European modernists, such as Picasso, Cézanne, Matisse, and Kandinsky, and also painters of the ASHCAN SCHOOL.

**armpit of the nation** a nickname for NEW JERSEY, because of its high pollution levels.

**Armstrong, Louis** 1900–1971. JAZZ musician. A towering figure in the history of jazz who invented many of its classic idioms, such as SWING. Over the years, he became a master improviser, an instrumental virtuoso, and a soloist who transcended traditional musical boundaries. His nickname was Satchmo.

**Arnold, Benedict** 1. 1741–1801. U.S. military officer who as commander of the fort at West Point, NEW YORK, conspired to turn it over to the British. 2. any traitor.

**Arthur, Chester** 1829–1886. Twenty-first president of the United States (1881–1885).

**Articles of Confederation** a 1781 agreement among the original THIRTEEN COLONIES outlining a weak federal government that lacked the authority to collect taxes. It was replaced by the CONSTITUTION in 1789.

**AS** TERRITORY OF AMERICAN SAMOA. (The official two-letter post office abbreviation.)

**ASCII** AMERICAN STANDARD CODE FOR INFORMATION INTERCHANGE.

**ASE** AMERICAN STOCK EXCHANGE.

**Ashcan School** a group of American artists, including John Sloan (1871–1951), Robert Henri (1865–1929), and George Bellows (1882–1925), noted for their realistic paintings of the seamy side of urban life.

**Asian** a person from Japan, China, the Philippines, Korea, or Vietnam, or a descendant of such a person.

**ASL** AMERICAN SIGN LANGUAGE.

**aspect ratio** the width-to-height ratio of a movie or television image.

**Associate in Arts** a two-year college degree. Abbreviated A.A.

**Associated Press** the oldest news agency in the United States, founded in 1848. It is also the largest worldwide press association. Abbreviated AP.

**Astaire, Fred** 1899–1987. Choreographer and dancer. One of the most popular entertainers of the mid-century, the debonair Astaire excelled in ballroom, tap, and ballet dancing. He moved easily from BROADWAY to HOLLYWOOD, where he became a star.

**AstroTurf** the trademarked name for artificial grass commonly used in FOOTBALL stadiums.

***Atlantic Monthly*** a literary magazine founded in Boston in 1857. Its first editor was JAMES RUSSELL LOWELL.

**ATM** automatic teller machine, an electronic machine owned by a bank, that dispenses cash.

**AT&T** American Telephone and Telegraph, an information processing and telecommunications company that provides communication products and services worldwide.

**Audubon, John James** 1785–1851. Naturalist and painter. His great work was a portfolio of more than 400 color engravings called *Birds of America*.

**Audubon Society** a conservationist society named after JOHN JAMES AUDUBON. The society's full name is National Audubon Society.

**Austin, Stephen F.** 1793–1836. Founder of the Republic of Texas and comrade-in-arms of SAMUEL HOUSTON in the Anglo revolt against Mexican dictator Antonio Lopez de Santa Anna.

**auteur** a filmmaker, usually a director, with a distinctive style.

**autofacturing** a blend of automation and manufacturing in which the entire assembly line is controlled by robots.

**Automat** a self-service restaurant in which coin-operated devices dispense cooked dishes.

**Avon lady** a saleswoman who sells Avon products, a trademarked brand of cosmetics and other products, door-to-door.

**AWOL** absent without leave; a military term for someone not present and not accounted for.

**AZ** ARIZONA. (The official two-letter post office abbreviation.)

**B.A.** BACHELOR OF ARTS.

***Babbitt*** 1. a novel by SINCLAIR LEWIS about a conformist who mindlessly follows popular standards and tastes (1922). 2. a conformist who mindlessly follows popular standards.

**baby boom** a surge in the births of babies, particularly in the immediate post-WORLD WAR II years. Those born in such a period are called *baby boomers* or *boomers*.

**baby boomer** See BABY BOOM.

**baby bust** the period after the end of a baby boom, generally after the mid-1960s. Those born in such a period are called *baby busters*. They are also regarded as members of GENERATION X.

**baby buster** See BABY BUST.

**bachelor** an unmarried man.

**Bachelor of Arts** a four-year college degree in liberal arts. Abbreviated B.A.

**Bachelor of Science** a four-year college degree in science. Abbreviated B.S.

**bachelorette** a single woman. The female form of bachelor.

**Badger State** WISCONSIN.

**badland** in the western states, a region with scanty vegetation where erosion has created fantastic sculptured formations.

**Baez, Joan** 1941–. Singer and songwriter. Baez was a pioneer of the FOLK REVIVAL and is a vigorous political activist.

**Balanchine, George** 1904–1983. Choreographer, born in Russia as Georgi Balanchivadze. He cofounded the New York City Ballet and choreographed over 200 works, the most important of which was *Apollon Musagete* (1928).

**bald eagle** a large North American eagle whose body is brown and head is white; it has been the national emblem of the United States since 1782.

**Baldwin, Roger Nash** 1884–1981. Civil liberties leader. Baldwin was the principal founder of the AMERICAN CIVIL LIBERTIES UNION and its director for the first 30 years.

**ballpark** a BASEBALL stadium.

**ballpark figure** a rough estimate.

*bald eagle*

**banana republic** a small dependent country, especially in the tropics. Used pejoratively.

**Bancroft, George** 1800–1891. Historian. Bancroft authored the 10-volume *History of the United States*, a two-volume history of the U.S. CONSTITUTION, and biographies of ABRAHAM LINCOLN and MARTIN VAN BUREN.

**bandwidth** 1. the spread between the upper and lower frequencies of a band of electromagnetic radiation, especially an assigned range of radio frequency. 2. the size of the data pipeline through which information passes in a network.

**banjo** a stringed musical instrument similar to a guitar, with a long neck and a circular body. Often used in BLUEGRASS, COUNTRY MUSIC, or FOLK MUSIC.

**banned in Boston**  puritanical efforts, typical of early NEW ENGLAND, to suppress or censor certain types of books and other artistic creations.

**Barbary Coast**  during the latter half of the 19th century, San Francisco, CALIFORNIA's lawless waterfront district. From the original Barbary Coast in Western North Africa.

**barbecue**  1. an outdoor grill used to cook food. 2. a party or meal where people eat food cooked on a grill. Barbecues are popular American events in the summertime. 3. the food that is prepared on an outdoor grill. It is usually covered with a spicy, tomato-based sauce. 4. to cook food on an outdoor grill. (Sometimes abbreviated BBQ.)

**Barbie**  the trademarked name of a dressed-up female doll introduced by Mattell in 1959. It is still highly popular today.

**barn dance**  a gathering, originally held in a barn, that includes square dancing and music.

**barnburner**  an uncommon event or situation.

**barnstorming**  a political campaign in which a candidate crisscrosses the country or state in search of votes.

**Barnum and Bailey**  America's premier circus company, originally formed in Somers, NEW YORK. Barnum and Bailey's extravagant shows, featuring Jumbo the elephant and General Tom Thumb, toured the United States as the GREATEST SHOW ON EARTH. It merged with the Ringling Brothers circus in 1907.

**Barnum, Phineas Taylor**  1810–1891. Circus impresario and showman. He, along with James A. Bailey, founded the Barnum and Bailey Circus. *The Life of P. T. Barnum* chronicles his life.

**Barrow, Clyde**  See BONNIE AND CLYDE.

*Bartlett's Familiar Quotations*  a book of quotations first compiled by John Bartlett (1820–1905), a Cambridge, MASSACHUSETTS, publisher, in 1855.

**Barton, Clarissa Harlowe (Clara)** 1821–1912. Founder of the American Red Cross. She was known as the "Angel of the Battlefield" for her humanitarian work as a nurse during the CIVIL WAR.

**baseball** 1. a national sport, dating from 1845, based in part on rules devised by Alexander Cartwright, founder of the first organized baseball club. Though it is widely disputed now, military officer Abner Doubleday (1819–1893) was once thought to be the inventor of the game. Baseball season runs from April to October. The game is played on a field by two teams of nine players and consists of nine INNINGS (or more, if the teams are tied at the end of the ninth inning). The objective is to score more runs than the opposing team. At the end of the baseball season, the first-place teams from each league, the AMERICAN LEAGUE and the NATIONAL LEAGUE, play for the championship in the WORLD SERIES. 2. the white leather-covered ball used in the game of baseball.

**Basie, Count** 1904–1984. Pianist and bandleader. Basie founded one of the major big bands of the SWING era.

**basketball** 1. a national sport developed in 1891 in Springfield, MASSACHUSETTS, by James Naismith (1861–1939), a YMCA physical education instructor. Basketball is played on a court by two teams of five players each, who score goals by sending a ball through a netted hoop, or a basket. A professional basketball game is separated into four quarters, each 12 minutes long. 2. the inflated ball used in the game of basketball.

**"Battle Hymn of the Republic, The"** a marching song of the UNION Army during the CIVIL WAR, based on the melody from an old religious song with lyrics by author Julia Ward Howe (1819–1910).

*Bay Psalm Book* the first book printed in the English colonies in 1640, a translation of the Book of Psalms in the Bible.

**Bay State** MASSACHUSETTS.

**bayou** a swampy, slow-moving stream, common in southern LOUISIANA.

**BBB** BETTER BUSINESS BUREAU.

**BBQ** BARBECUE.

**Beacon Hill** the home of Boston's elite families.

**bean counter** an unimaginative official who performs routine chores, such as keeping records.

**Beantown** a nickname for Boston, MASSACHUSETTS, from its traditional dish of baked beans.

**bear market** a market in which the falling prices of stocks are yielding poor profits.

**Beat Generation** the countercultural literary group that included the poets LAWRENCE FERLINGHETTI and ALLEN GINSBERG and novelists WILLIAM S. BURROUGHS and JACK KEROUAC. The folk etymology of Beat Generation is from *beatific*.

**beatnik** a member of the BEAT GENERATION or one of its followers.

**beauty contest** a primary election practice in which delegates are selected by party caucuses rather than voters.

**Beaver State** OREGON.

**bebop** a 1940s style of JAZZ exhibiting lean rhythms, innovative harmonies, and fast improvisations. Its principal exponents were THELONIOUS MONK, DIZZY GILLESPIE, and CHARLIE "BIRD" PARKER.

**bee** 1. a gathering of people for the collective performance of a task, such as husking or quilting. 2. a competitive quiz program, such as a spelling bee.

**Beecher, Henry Ward** 1813–1887. Religious leader. As the son of clergyman Lyman Beecher (1775–1863) and pastor of the Plymouth Congregational Church in Brooklyn, Beecher was one of the most influential ministers of the 19th century.

**beefalo** beef cattle developed through crossbreeding domestic cattle and buffalo.

**Beehive State** UTAH.

**Belasco, David** 1854–1931. Actor, dramatist, and producer. Known as the Bishop of Broadway, Belasco played over 200 roles as an actor, but was better known as an excellent stage manager and promoter of talent.

**Bell, Alexander Graham** 1847–1922. Inventor of the telephone. Born in Scotland, Bell was a teacher of the deaf. His words to his assistant, "Mr. Watson, come here, I want you," on March 10, 1876, were the first be to be carried over wires, and they launched the age of modern communications.

**bell lap** the final lap of a race, signaled by the sounding of a bell.

**Bell Telephone Company** an arm of AT&T. Bell once monopolized the U.S. telephone industry. Nicknamed *Ma Bell*.

*Alexander Graham Bell*

**Bellamy, Edward** 1850–1898. Reformer and futurist. His visionary work, *Looking Backward*, inspired many utopian movements.

**Bellow, Saul** 1915–. Novelist. Bellow has won the Nobel Prize for Literature and three National Book Awards for a series of extraordinary novels, including *The Adventures of Augie March* (1953), *Henderson the Rain King* (1959), and *Mr. Sammler's Planet* (1970).

**Bellows, George** 1882–1925. Painter. Bellows, who painted urban scenes, helped to mount the 1913 ARMORY SHOW.

**Beltway** the U.S. federal government. The beltway is the circular road that runs around the city of WASHINGTON, D.C.

**Beltway Bandit** a WASHINGTON, D.C., lobbyist, consultant, or influence peddler.

**Benet, Stephen Vincent** 1898–1943. Poet and writer. Benet authored the story "The Devil and Daniel Webster" and the poem *John Brown's Body*, both of which won the PULITZER PRIZE.

**Benny, Jack** 1894–1974. Comedian. Born Benjamin Kubelsky, he began working on radio in the 1930s and then moved into movies and television. He is considered a master comedian who made the pregnant pause and deadpan delivery into an art form.

**Benton, Thomas Hart** 1889–1975. Painter. Benton painted realistic dramatic scenes of life in the American heartland.

**Bergen, Edgar** 1903–1978. Ventriloquist. Bergen's dummy, the wisecracking Charlie McCarthy, is now in the SMITHSONIAN INSTITUTION.

**Berlin, Irving** 1888–1989. Songwriter. Born Isidore Baline in Russia, he dominated American popular music for 40 years until the 1970s.

**Bernstein, Leonard** 1918–1990. Composer and conductor. He was director of the New York Philharmonic from 1958 to 1969 and created the scores for *On the Town* and *West Side Story*.

**Berry, Chuck** 1926–. Pioneering ROCK AND ROLL musician. His songwriting ability and guitar riffs have inspired many rock musicians.

**Berryman, John** 1914–1972. Poet. Despair and loss of hope were common themes in his poetry, which was often marked by vivid imagery and inverted syntax.

**Bettelheim, Bruno** 1903–1990. Psychologist. A pioneer in the treatment of psychological problems of children and adolescents, his methods were sometimes effective and sometimes controversial.

**Better Business Bureau** an organization that monitors business activities and alerts and protects consumers from fraud. Abbreviated BBB.

**Bible Belt** Southern states as a region characterized by strong adherence to Christian and biblical values.

**Big Apple** a nickname for New York City. Folk etymology is from the jazz term, apple, for city.

**Big Band** a large band, usually one that plays SWING. Big Bands were very popular in the 1940s.

**Big Blue** a nickname for IBM.

**Big Ditch** a nickname for the ERIE CANAL or the Panama Canal.

**Big Easy** a nickname for New Orleans, LOUISIANA, from the alleged availability of easy women in the city.

**big government** the federal government, as a bloated organization that intrudes, through its various agencies and legal codes, into the private lives of the citizens and regulates all aspects of their lives.

**Big Muddy** a nickname for the MISSISSIPPI RIVER.

**big stick** toughness in dealing with foreign nations and aggressiveness in promoting national interests. From THEODORE ROOSEVELT's motto: Speak Softly and Carry a Big Stick.

**bigfoot** SASQUATCH.

**bikeway** a road on which only bicycles are permitted.

**Bill of Rights** the first 10 amendments to the U.S. CONSTITUTION, which affirm the personal liberties granted by the U.S. Constitution.

*Billy the Kid*

**Billy the Kid** 1859–1891. Outlaw. Born William H. Bonney, he was the OLD WEST's most notorious desperado, who reportedly boasted that he had killed one person for every year of his life.

**bingo** a game of chance, popular as a fundraising activity in churches and synagogues. As numbers are called out, a player covers the numbers on a printed card with markers. When a player has a complete line of markers, he or she shouts "bingo."

**biodegradable** able to be decomposed by biological agents, especially bacteria.

**biodiversity** the diversity of plant and animal species in a given ecological region, considered as a desirable goal in the management of the environment.

**Biosphere** a man-made, sealed, sphere-like structure, resembling a greenhouse, designed for self-sustaining existence by human beings for a specified period of time.

*Birth of a Nation, The* a silent film produced by D. W. GRIFFITH in 1915, considered as the first great movie epic.

**biscuit** a small round of baked dough, usually leavened with baking powder.

**Bishop of Broadway** DAVID BELASCO.

**black belt** the highest symbol of proficiency in judo or karate.

**Black English** a dialect of English as spoken and written by AFRICAN-AMERICANS that varies from standard English and includes many peculiarities of pronunciation and grammar. See EBONICS.

**black flag** a flag used in race tracks to signal a race car driver to leave the course.

**Black Friday** September 24, 1869, when the financial markets collapsed following illegal transactions by ROBBER BARONS Jay Gould and James Fisk.

**Black History Month** the month of February, dedicated to a heightened awareness of the history and achievements of AFRICAN-AMERICANS.

**black humor** humor derived from ludicrous or absurd situations with undertones of sadness.

**Black Is Beautiful** slogan of the BLACK POWER MOVEMENT, first used in the 1920s by MARCUS GARVEY.

*Black Mask* premier pulp magazine, founded in 1920 by H. L. MENCKEN and GEORGE JEAN NATHAN, that specialized in hard-boiled fiction and launched the careers of DASHIELL HAMMETT and RAYMOND CHANDLER.

**Black Muslims** the popular term for the Nation of Islam, a Muslim sect founded in 1930 in Detroit. It is hostile to whites in general and Jews in particular, and advocates a separate black nation. Black Muslims were led in the 1960s by MALCOLM X.

**Black Panthers** a militant black organization of the 1960s and 1970s. Among its members were activists Huey Newton (1942–1988) and Eldridge Cleaver (1935–). Its slogan was BLACK POWER.

**Black Power** the slogan adopted by the BLACK PANTHERS.

**Black Power Movement** an AFRICAN-AMERICAN activist movement of the 1960s that developed from the CIVIL RIGHTS MOVEMENT. The movement emphasized the progress of blacks through independent social and political organization, sometimes using force.

**Black Tuesday** October 29, 1929, when the stock market collapsed as a prelude to the GREAT DEPRESSION.

**blackjack** TWENTY-ONE.

**Blair House** the official VIP guest house in WASHINGTON, D.C.

**blind date** a date for two people that is arranged by a third person; an arranged rendezvous for two people who have never met.

**Block, Herbert Lawrence** 1909–. Editorial cartoonist. Under the pen name *Herblock*, Block was the scourge of errant politicians for more than four decades.

**blockbuster** a best-selling book or a movie that is aggressively promoted.

**bloomers** Turkish style women's pantaloons, worn with a short skirt. So called after Amelia Jenks Bloomer (1818–1894), feminist editor.

**BLT** a bacon, lettuce, and tomato sandwich. It is usually made on toast and includes mayonnaise.

**blue helmet** a member of the United Nations peacekeeping force sent to various countries to keep warring factions apart.

**blue law** any of several laws prohibiting certain secular activities on the Christian sabbath on Sunday; so called because the laws were originally printed on blue paper. One such law, which still survives in some areas, restricts commercial sales on Sunday.

**blue-collar** describing employees who do manual or physical work, as opposed to those in professional occupations (see WHITE-

COLLAR). They are so called because many wear blue uniforms or other special work clothing.

**bluegrass** traditional COUNTRY MUSIC, pioneered by Bill Monroe, that is a combination of GOSPEL MUSIC and folk melodies. It is played with a rich range of instruments, including BANJOS, guitars, mandolins, and fiddles, and is characterized by plaintive high harmonies, a driving rhythm, and virtuoso string work.

**Bluegrass State** KENTUCKY.

**blues** an AFRICAN-AMERICAN musical form that is generally melancholic and characterized by three-line stanzas, eight- or 12-bar structure, and JAZZ rhythm. It is usually in a major key with the third and seventh (the blue notes) flatted optionally. Growing out of the work songs of slaves, the blues evolved in several styles, of which the most prominent are the DELTA BLUES and amplified blues.

**boards** the stage in a theater.

**boardwalk** a wooden promenade, as in the Atlantic City, NEW JERSEY, oceanfront.

**Boas, Franz** 1858–1942. Anthropologist. German-born Boas was one of the founding fathers of anthropology in the United States. Much of his scientific research was concentrated on the Indians of the northwest coast of British Columbia, particularly the Kwakiutl tribe of Vancouver. Among his many published works is the classic *Handbook of American Indian Languages*.

**boatel** a hotel in a marina for use by boat owners or passengers.

**body bag** a rubberized and zippered bag in which corpses are transported.

**body language** subconscious means of communication through gestures and postures apart from or in addition to speech.

**boffo** the male singer of comic opera roles.

**Bonnie and Clyde** a team of criminals, Bonnie Parker (1910–1934) and Clyde Barrow (1909–1934), who were responsible for several murders and bank robberies in the 1930s. They were finally killed in a shootout with police.

**booboisie** the intellectually challenged members of the American bourgeoisie. Coined by H. L. MENCKEN from boob, a simpleton.

**boogie** a fast and lively form of ROCK AND ROLL based on the BLUES.

**boogie-woogie** a style of JAZZ piano in which the bass is marked by repeated melodic and rhythmic patterns and the treble by a series of improvisations.

**book packaging** the production of a book by a book producer who sells it to a publisher for publication under the latter's imprint.

**boom** a movable arm that holds a microphone over the heads of actors during filming.

**boombox** a large radio or tape player with powerful speakers.

**boomer** See BABY BOOM.

**boomerang baby** a young person, usually employed, who leaves home, only to come back to live with his or her parents.

**Boone, Daniel** 1734–1820. Folk hero and frontiersman. Boone helped to open the Trans-Appalachian West to white expansion by cutting the Wilderness Road through the CUMBERLAND GAP in 1775.

**boot camp** the training camp for U.S. Marines or Navy recruits.

**Booth, Edwin** 1833–1893. Shakespearean actor and tragedian. He was noted for his role as the brooding Hamlet and was the brother of JOHN WILKES BOOTH.

**Booth, John Wilkes** 1838–1865. Actor and assassin of President ABRAHAM LINCOLN. Brother of EDWIN BOOTH.

**bop** a complex JAZZ style in which the solo performance is marked by free improvisation.

**born again** a scriptural conversion experience in which a Christian is spiritually born into the kingdom of God with a renewed personal commitment to Christ and is empowered by the Holy Spirit to do His will. From the Gospel of John 3.3 and 3.7, where Jesus mandates such a conversion.

**Borscht Belt** a resort area in NEW YORK's Catskill Mountains frequented by Jewish vacationers from New York City.

**Boston Brahmin** a member of one of Boston's elite families, described by OLIVER WENDELL HOLMES as "the harmless, inoffensive and untitled aristocracy."

**Boston Tea Party** 1773 protest by American colonists against the tea tax imposed by the British government. A group of Americans dressed up as INDIANS, boarded a British tea company's ship, and threw the British tea overboard into Boston Harbor.

**bottom line** the overall profit or loss, as noted in the last line of an annual financial statement.

**bourbon** American whiskey, made of corn, malt and rye, named after Bourbon County, KENTUCKY, where it was originally made.

**Bow, Clara** 1905–1965. Actress. Popular during the silent cinema era, Bow epitomized the young American woman of her time and was nicknamed the *It Girl*.

**Bowery** a New York City street, noted as the SKID ROW. So called from the fact that the street originally led to the Dutch governor's farm, or *bouverie*.

**bowl** a FOOTBALL stadium, as the Rose Bowl in CALIFORNIA, Orange Bowl in Miami, Sugar Bowl in New Orleans, and Cotton Bowl in Dallas.

**Boy Orator of the Platte** nickname of WILLIAM JENNINGS BRYAN, U.S. Representative from NEBRASKA (1891–1895), from the Platte River, which runs through that state.

**Boys Town** a settlement for homeless and delinquent boys established by Father Edward Flanagan (1886–1948), a Catholic priest, in Omaha, NEBRASKA.

**bps** bits per second, the rate at which data travel between modems.

**Bradford, William** 1590–1657. PILGRIM leader and colonial governor. Bradford helped to found PLYMOUTH COLONY.

**Brady Bill** legislation outlawing or restricting the sale of certain types of handguns and other lethal weapons. From Jim Brady, former aide to President RONALD REAGAN, who was shot and disabled by an assailant during an assassination attempt on the president.

**Brady, Mathew B.** 1823–1896. Photographer known for his photographs of the CIVIL WAR era. His *Gallery of Illustrious Americans* is the first major collection of American portraits.

**brain drain** the large-scale flight of talented personnel, such as scientists and doctors, from developing countries to developed countries in search of better job opportunities.

**Brain Trust** 1. the inner circle of advisers who helped President FRANKLIN DELANO ROOSEVELT to shepherd the NEW DEAL programs. 2. (usually lowercased) any group of intellectual advisers.

**Brandeis, Louis Dembitz** 1856–1941. Jurist. The first Jew on the U.S. SUPREME COURT, Brandeis served as an associate justice from 1916 to 1939 and made significant contributions to advancing social reform, social legislation, and liberal interpretation of the CONSTITUTION.

**brass** high-ranking members of the military. Also, *top brass*.

**Brewster, William** 1567–1644. PILGRIM leader. Brewster was one of the founders of PLYMOUTH COLONY.

**broadcast fax** the sending of fax messages simultaneously to multiple recipients.

**broadcast journalism** news reporting for radio and television. Also called *electronic journalism*. Distinguished from print journalism.

**Broadway** 1. a New York City thoroughfare used metaphorically as a synonym for the theatrical-entertainment industry. 2. of or pertaining to the theater and entertainment district of Broadway.

**brokered convention** a convention where the candidates are chosen by party leaders rather than by rank-and-file delegates.

**Bronx cheer** a derisive sound made by protruding the tongue and blowing hard through pursed lips. Also known as a *raspberry*.

**Brook Farm** utopian community in West Roxbury, MASSACHUSETTS (1841–1847), founded by transcendentalist George Ripley (1802–1880). Newspaper editor Charles Dana (1819–1897) and NATHANIEL HAWTHORNE were once members of this farm.

**Brooklyn Bridge** a suspension bridge, at one time the world's longest, between MANHATTAN and Brooklyn, two boroughs of New York City. It was completed in 1883.

**Brooklynese** the dialect of Brooklyn, New York City, characterized by the use of *oi* for *er*, *d* for *th*, and dropped *r*'s.

*Brooklyn Bridge*

**Brother Jonathan** in Colonial times, personification of the rustic Yankee or New Englander. It was eventually replaced by UNCLE SAM.

**brown bag** 1. a brown paper bag used to carry bottles of liquor, generally secretively. 2. to carry one's lunch in a brown bag.

**Brown Bomber** JOE LOUIS.

**Brown, Helen Gurley** 1922–. Author and editor. Brown, once one of the most influential women in the country, is best known as the editor of *Cosmopolitan* magazine. Her book *Sex and the Single Girl* (1962) was considered controversial.

**Brown, John** 1800–1859. Abolitionist. He helped to spark the CIVIL WAR with his raid on Harper's Ferry, VIRGINIA, and seizure of armaments for the abolitionist cause.

**brown thumb** a lack of innate gardening skills, considered as a physical trait. The opposite of a GREEN THUMB.

**Brown University** an IVY LEAGUE university in Providence, RHODE ISLAND, that opened in 1764 as Rhode Island College.

***Brown v. Board of Education*** the landmark 1954 case in which the SUPREME COURT struck down segregation in public schools, thus opening the door to desegregation in a number of areas of public life.

**browser** a program that permits WORLD WIDE WEB users to download and display documents.

**Bryan, William Jennings** 1860–1925. Political leader. Perhaps best known for assisting the prosecution at the famous SCOPES TRIAL, Bryan had a colorful political career. Known for his speaking skill, he was nicknamed *Boy Orator of the Platte* while he served as a U.S. Representative from Nebraska. His stirring "Cross of Gold" speech at the Democratic National Convention of 1896, in which he criticized the gold standard, resulted in a nomination for president by the DEMOCRATIC PARTY. He was nominated a total of three times, gathering a substantial number of votes, but lost each time.

**Bryant, William Cullen** 1794–1878. Abolitionist and long-time editor of the *New York Evening Post*. Bryant's editorials helped to fan the flames of discontent and mobilize public opposition to slavery.

**Bryce Canyon** a national park in southern UTAH. It was established in 1928 and is known for the spectacular colored walls of its box canyon.

**B.S.** BACHELOR OF SCIENCE.

**bubba** a Southern male (generally pejorative).

**bubbletop** the dome-shaped, transparent, bulletproof roof of an automobile carrying important public officials, designed to protect them against assassination attempts.

**Buchanan, James** 1791–1868. Fifteenth president of the United States (1857–1861).

**Buck, Pearl** 1892–1973. Novelist. Buck is best known for her novels about China, especially *The Good Earth*, for which she won a PULITZER PRIZE in 1932. Buck received the Nobel Prize for Literature in 1938.

**Buckeye State** OHIO.

**Buckley, William, Jr.** 1925–. Editor and writer. A leading conservative described as the conscience of the Right, Buckley was a founder and long-time editor of the *National Review*. He is also noted as a word MAVEN.

**Bud** Budweiser, a popular trademarked brand of beer.

**Buffalo Bill** 1846–1917. Frontiersman and showman. Born William Frederick Cody, in early life he rode for the PONY EXPRESS and shot buffalo for the Kansas Pacific Railroad. In 1883 he organized the famous WILD WEST SHOW.

**buffalo wings** chicken wings cooked in a spicy sauce, usually served with raw celery sticks and a creamy dipping sauce. Named for the city of Buffalo, NEW YORK, where they originated.

**Bulfinch, Charles** 1763–1844. Architect. He developed the FEDERAL STYLE, designed the CONNECTICUT and MASSACHUSETTS statehouses, and completed the work on the U.S. CAPITOL after the departure of Benjamin Latrobe.

**bull market** a market in which rising prices of stocks are yielding strong profits.

**Bull Moose Party** a nickname for the Progressive Party organized by THEODORE ROOSEVELT after he lost the Republican nomination to WILLIAM HOWARD TAFT in 1912. Derived from Roosevelt's standard remark that he was fit as a bull moose.

**bullcrit** critical discussion of a book or play on the basis of hearsay without actually reading or seeing it.

**bullet vote** balloting in which the electorate concentrates on a single candidate or issue to the exclusion of others.

**bullpen** 1. a place where bulls are kept or raised. 2. the area on a BASEBALL field where players practice before going onto the field.

**bully pulpit** THEODORE ROOSEVELT's description of the presidency as a forum for edifying the American public.

**Bunche, Ralph Johnson** 1904–1971. Public servant. The first AFRICAN-AMERICAN to win the Nobel Peace Prize in 1950, Bunche was a senior United Nations official who led peacekeeping efforts in troubled areas.

**bungee jumping** a sport in which a person using an ankle harness jumps from a high platform, such as a bridge, hot-air balloon, or crane, to which he or she is tied by elastic cords. The elastic action of the cords allows free fall up to a point, after which the person bounces like a yo-yo.

**Burbank, Luther** 1849–1926. Horticulturist. Burbank produced hundreds of new varieties of fruits, plants, and flowers against the objections of religious fundamentalists.

**burlesque** a form of theater characterized by low humor and striptease.

**Burma Shave** doggerel couplets, set at intervals on boards along the highways, before the rise of interstate highways. They were part of an advertising campaign by a shaving cream company.

**burnout** depletion of energy, motivation, and drive, especially as a result of excessive exertion and devotion to work.

**Burr, Aaron** 1756–1836. Politician and third vice president of the United States (1801–1805). Burr is best remembered for his ongoing conflict with rival ALEXANDER HAMILTON, whom he killed in a duel in 1804.

**Burroughs, Edgar Rice** 1875–1950. Novelist. He is best known as the creator of TARZAN in his novel *Tarzan of the Apes* and the author of more than 70 books dealing with jungle adventures.

**Burroughs, William S.** 1914–1997. Novelist. Burroughs, a member of the BEAT GENERATION and a heroin addict, is known for his novels that deal with drug addiction, most notably *The Naked Lunch* (1959).

**Bush, George** 1924–. Forty-first president of the United States (1989–1993).

**busing** the transportation of school students by buses to schools outside their school districts to achieve racial balance, particularly to redress the heavy concentration of African-American students in inner-city schools.

**busway** a lane in a public highway set apart for public transportation.

**Butler, Nicholas Murray** 1862–1947. Educator and peace activist. As president of COLUMBIA UNIVERSITY (1902–1945), Butler made it one of the topflight institutions in the country. He helped to found the Carnegie Endowment for International Peace and was the architect of the Kellogg-Briand Pact of 1927 outlawing war.

33

**butte** in the Western states, an isolated, flat-topped hill with steep sides.

**button-down** conventional and conservative, tied down to routine, and seeking safety in the commonplace.

**BYOB** bring your own bottle. A party for which food is provided, but where those invited are expected to bring any alcohol or other beverage they may wish to drink. BYOB is usually written on the invitation.

**CA** CALIFORNIA. (The official two-letter post office abbreviation.)

**cable car** a vehicle moved by motor-driven cables along city streets. Once common in all large cities, the cable car is now found only in San Francisco, CALIFORNIA.

**cablecast** to telecast by cable television.

*cable car*

**Cadillac** the top of the line in any product group, from the trademarked name of the luxury automobile.

**Caesar's Palace** a famous hotel/casino/entertainment venue on THE STRIP in Las Vegas, NEVADA.

**Cajun** 1. a resident of LOUISIANA descended from French colonists deported by the British from Nova Scotia (Acadia in French) in 1755. Cajuns have a very distinctive cuisine and music. 2. of or relating to the culture of the Cajuns.

**Calder, Alexander Sterling** 1898–1976. Sculptor. By incorporating motion into sculpture, he created a new 20th-century art form called mobiles and stationary sculptures called stabiles.

**California** a state in the western United States, bordered on the west by the Pacific Ocean. Called the Golden State, its capital is Sacramento and its largest city is Los Angeles. It is the most populated state in the country. The state bird is the California valley quail and the state flower is the golden poppy. Abbreviated CA.

**California gold rush**  the influx of prospectors to California after the discovery of gold there in 1848.

**calligram**  a poem in which the lines are arranged in the form of a picture representing the subject of the poem. Thus a poem about a Christmas tree will appear as a Christmas tree.

**call-in**  a radio or television program where listeners phone in live comments or questions to the show's host or his or her guests. Also *phone-in*.

**calypso**  1. West Indian music with improvised lyrics. 2. a West Indian dance accompanied by lively music.

**Camelot**  an idyllic place in England in the time of King Arthur, filled with heroic exploits. Applied nostalgically to the administration of President JOHN FITZGERALD KENNEDY.

**camel's nose**  something difficult and unpleasant that could possibly bring in its wake something even more difficult or unmanageable.

**Camp David**  the presidential retreat in the Catoctin Mountains of MARYLAND, originally built for FRANKLIN DELANO ROOSEVELT.

**Camp Fire Girls**  a recreational organization for girls founded in 1910 by Luther and Charlotte Gulick. The name was changed to Camp Fire Boys and Girls after boys were admitted in the 1970s.

**camp meeting**  an open-air religious meeting of the early 1800s, the equivalent of a modern crusade. Such meetings were instrumental in promoting the GREAT REVIVAL and in spreading evangelical Christianity in frontier towns.

**canned**  describing material recorded and stored for repeated use on television and radio, such as canned laughter or canned applause.

**Cape Cod**  a sandy peninsula southeast of MASSACHUSETTS extending east from the mainland and forming a wide curve near the north enclosing the Cape Cod Bay.

**capitol**  a building in which a state legislature meets.

**Capitol** the building in which the U.S. CONGRESS meets, located in WASHINGTON MALL in WASHINGTON, D.C.

**Capitol Hill** 1. the site of the CAPITOL, where CONGRESS meets. 2. the U.S. CONGRESS.

*the Capitol*

**Capone, Al** 1899–1947. Organized-crime boss. Born in Italy, Capone began his criminal career in New York and later became leader of the MOB in Chicago, ILLINOIS, during PROHIBITION. Nicknamed *Scarface*, he amassed great wealth from his bootlegging organization, routinely ordering the execution of his rivals (see ST. VALENTINE'S DAY MASSACRE). Never convicted for bootlegging or murder, Capone was finally found guilty of tax evasion and jailed.

*Al Capone*

**Capote, Truman** 1924–1984. Journalist and novelist. One of the founders of the nonfiction novel. His *In Cold Blood* is a classic account of a multiple murder on a KANSAS farm.

**Capri pants** tight-fitting women's trousers, worn on informal occasions. Originally from the isle of Capri in Italy.

**capture** to retrieve information stored in a computer or data bank.

**car pool** a group of commuters who regularly take turns driving each other to work or for other purposes.

**card-carrying** describing a full-fledged, registered member of a party or group.

**CARE** Cooperative for American Relief in Europe, a charity organization that sent packages of food and clothes to the needy after WORLD WAR II.

**caregiver**  a person who looks after the very sick or elderly who are unable to care for themselves.

**carjacking**  the armed theft of an automobile (patterned on hijacking).

**Carlsbad Caverns National Park**  a national park in southeast NEW MEXICO established in 1930. The park contains miles of limestone caves with remarkable formations.

**Carnegie, Andrew**  1835–1919. Industrialist and philanthropist. At one time, he was the richest man in the world. Carnegie rose from rags to riches by sheer industry and financial acumen to become the founder of the Carnegie Steel Company, which he sold to the United States Steel Corporation for $350 million in 1901. Thereafter, he devoted all of his wealth to philanthropy.

**Carnegie Hall**  a famous concert hall in New York City, known for its excellent acoustics. It was named after ANDREW CARNEGIE.

**carpetbagger**  a corrupt agent of the federal government charged with the enforcement of RECONSTRUCTION policies in the SOUTH after the CIVIL WAR. So called because they carried their belongings in carpet-covered bags.

**Carson, Kit**  1809–1868. Frontiersman. Born Christopher Carson, he was a skilled and courageous guide for several expeditions. In 1854 he was appointed as a U.S. Indian agent and soon gained fame as an Indian fighter.

**Carson, Rachel**  1907–1964. Marine biologist and ecologist. Her books, *The Sea Around Us* (1951) and *The Silent Spring* (1962), in which she questioned the use of pesticides, helped to launch the environmental revolution.

**Carter, Jimmy**  1924–. Thirty-ninth president of the United States (1977–1981).

**Carver, George Washington**  1864–1943. Botanist and educator. Carver worked at the Tuskegee Institute (now TUSKEGEE UNIVERSITY) in Macon County in ALABAMA. He developed patents for many new methods of growing and using agricultural products such as peanuts.

**cascade effect**  a chain of events where each episode causes or intensifies the next. Compare DOMINO EFFECT.

**Cascade Range**  a mountain range near the west coast of the United States across OREGON and WASHINGTON. It includes MOUNT SAINT HELENS, and its highest peak is Mount Rainier (14,410 ft).

**cash cow**  an enterprise that provides regular and dependable income or profit but which requires little effort or investment in return.

**casket**  a coffin.

**catch-22**  an illogical situation or problem that presents two equally undesirable solutions that are contradicted by the nature of the problem. From Joseph Heller's popular novel of the same name.

**Cather, Willa**  1873–1947. Novelist. Cather is noted for her classic historic novels, *My Antonia* (1918) and *Death Comes for the Archbishop* (1927).

**cattle show**  in a political primary, the public assembly of all candidates to enable voters to compare their strengths and weaknesses and assess their prospects.

**CB**  citizens band, a radio band used by private citizens.

**CBS**  the Columbia Broadcasting System, one of the three major television networks in the United States, along with ABC and NBC. Headquartered in New York, it was incorporated in 1927 and also owns radio, news, entertainment, and sports affiliates. All three networks suffered losses of viewers with the advent of cable television, videocassette rentals, and new networks in the 1980s and 1990s.

**CCC**  Civilian Conservation Corps, a NEW DEAL program that put young men to work on public construction projects.

**CD**  certificate of deposit, a fixed-term financial instrument that yields a higher rate of interest than regular bank deposits.

**CDC**  CENTERS FOR DISEASE CONTROL.

**CDT**  CENTRAL DAYLIGHT TIME.

**Centennial State** COLORADO.

**centerfold** a two-page spread of a nubile woman or attractive man, generally unclad, that is folded at the middle of a magazine or book.

**Centers for Disease Control** founded in 1946 and now a part of the DEPARTMENT OF HEALTH AND HUMAN SERVICES, it protects and promotes health and wellness by overseeing programs for the prevention and control of disease, providing health information, conducting research, and developing immunization programs. Abbreviated CDC.

**central casting** the casting department of a studio, charged with the selection of actors. Used in the expression "straight from central casting" to signify something stereotypical.

**central city** historically, the nucleus of a city that is abandoned by more affluent residents who move to the suburbs and, as a result, is generally run down and inhabited by the poorest. Also *inner city*, *core city*.

**central daylight time** the adjusted time in the central United States during early April to late October. It is five hours behind Greenwich time. Abbreviated CDT.

**Central Intelligence Agency** the principal government agency concerned with gathering of foreign intelligence and the conduct of covert operations abroad. It was created by the National Security Act of 1947. Commonly abbreviated as CIA.

**Central Park** a large park located in MANHATTAN, New York City. Among its features are a zoo, an outdoor concert mall, and a conservatory garden.

**central standard time** the time in the central region of the United States from the last weekend in October to the first weekend in April. It is six hours behind Greenwich time. Abbreviated CST.

**Certified Public Accountant** an accountant who has met requirements as determined by the examining board of a particular state. Abbreviated CPA.

**Chairman of the Board** FRANK SINATRA.

**Chandler, Raymond** 1888–1959. Novelist and screenwriter. Chandler specialized in detective novels with streetwise characters. Among his works is *Farewell, My Lovely* (1940).

**channel** a medium or person through whom invisible beings or spirits supposedly communicate to people.

**channel surfing** the practice of scanning a series of television channels with the use of remote controls.

**chapbook** a popular form of literature that flourished in the United States from 1725 to 1825. Chapbooks were generally of small size, written by anonymous authors, and printed on cheap paper.

**Chaplin, Charlie** 1889–1977. Film actor, director, and producer. Born in England, he came to the United States in 1910. By 1918 he was the most popular film star in the world, specializing in slapstick comedy and developing an inimitable acting style marked by a wide range of facial expressions. Among his notable films were *The Kid* (1921), *The Gold Rush* (1925), *City Lights* (1931), *Modern Times* (1936), and *The Great Dictator* (1940).

**Charismatic** a Pentecostal Christian who believes in the charismatic gifts as outlined in the Epistles of St. Paul and as demonstrated on the day of the Pentecost. These gifts include speaking in tongues, healing by laying on of hands, and exorcism of evil spirits.

**Charleston** a dance style popular in the 1920s marked by swinging arms and kicking heels.

**Charter Oak** a landmark tree in Hartford, CONNECTICUT, where, in 1687, colonists are said to have hidden an antiroyalist charter from an official of the British government authorized to suspend it. Winds blew the tree down in 1856.

**Chautauqua Movement** a public education movement consisting of lectures, entertainment, correspondence courses, and traveling tent shows. An institute for this type of education was founded in Chautauqua, NEW YORK, in 1874. The movement was strong until the 1920s.

**Chavez, Cesar** 1927–1993. Labor leader. Against great odds, Chavez organized the first Chicano labor union of grape pickers in CALIFORNIA.

**checkbook journalism** journalism as practiced by mass-circulation tabloids that pay large sums of money to celebrities to obtain exclusive rights to personal stories or scandals.

**checkoff** a provision in a tax return for making a voluntary contribution to a specified cause or program.

**cheeseburger** a popular American sandwich, consisting of a patty of ground beef on a special bun topped with a slice of cheese and usually other ingredients; a HAMBURGER with cheese.

**Cherokee** one of the FIVE CIVILIZED TRIBES, evicted from their homeland in GEORGIA and force-marched to OKLAHOMA in the 1830s on a trek known as the TRAIL OF TEARS.

**Cheyenne** a NATIVE AMERICAN tribe who were buffalo hunters in the GREAT PLAINS. The state capital of WYOMING is named after them.

**Chicago school of architecture** the architectural movement that introduced the skyscraper. It began in Chicago, ILLINOIS, in the late 1800s, when architects began building with steel beams and masonry floors and walls after the Great Chicago Fire of 1871 destroyed hundreds of wooden framed buildings. One of its chief architects was LOUIS SULLIVAN.

**Chicago-style** (of a pizza) having a thick crust. (Popular in Chicago, ILLINOIS.)

**Chicana** See CHICANO.

**Chicano** a term applied to Mexican Americans. (Feminine is *Chicana*.)

**Chief Executive** the president of the United States.

**chili** a stew made of beans, tomatoes, ground beef, and hot spices.

**China Syndrome** a hypothetical meltdown in a nuclear plant resulting in a hole through the middle of the earth to the antipodes.

**Chinatown**  a section of a city, especially New York City and San Francisco, CALIFORNIA, inhabited mostly by Chinese.

**Chisholm Trail**  a cattle trail from TEXAS to Abilene, KANSAS, in the 1860s and 1870s, named for the Indian trader Jesse Chisholm. It was memorialized in the cowboy song "The Old Chisholm Trail."

**chitlins**  intestines of hogs, popular among AFRICAN-AMERICANS as SOUL food.

**Chomsky, (Avram) Noam**  1928–. Linguist. Chomsky made one of the most significant discoveries in linguistics, called transformational grammar. He is also a political activist noted for his lifelong opposition to the U.S. government's conduct of foreign relations.

**chop suey**  literally, bits and pieces. A Chinese-American dish invented in the West, consisting of bean sprouts, water chestnuts, bamboo shoots, and slivers of meat.

**chopper**  1. a helicopter. 2. to fly by helicopter.

**chow mein**  a Chinese-American dish of meat and assorted vegetables served on fried noodles.

**chowder**  a thick soup made with clams, other seafood, or vegetables. The New England version is a thick, milky broth with herbs and salt pork, while the Manhattan variety is a thin, reddish broth made with tomatoes.

**Christian Science**  a semi-Christian denomination founded in MASSACHUSETTS by MARY BAKER EDDY whose cardinal tenet is the spiritual healing of believers.

**Christmas tree**  a legislative bill to which numerous benefits are added by special-interest groups even though they have nothing to do with the main subject. These benefits are generally the result of wheeling-dealing among the legislators.

**chutzpah**  brazen audacity or impudence in claiming or doing something that violates good sense. From Yiddish *hutzpah*.

**CIA**  CENTRAL INTELLIGENCE AGENCY.

**cigar store Indian** formerly, a wooden Indian displayed outside a tobacco or other store as an advertising symbol. Now considered demeaning to Native Americans.

**Cinderella services** social services provided by public or private agencies to the poor, the needy, the aged, and the sick.

**cineaste** a film buff or movie enthusiast.

**cinema verité** a style of filmmaking marked by strong realism, often containing unedited sequences.

**CINS** children in need of supervision, a category of children prone to trouble if left without adult supervision.

**CIO** Congress of Industrial Nations. See AFL-CIO.

**City of Brotherly Love** Philadelphia, PENNSYLVANIA, from the literal rendering of the Greek name.

**City of the Angels** Los Angeles, CALIFORNIA.

**civil religion** the quasi-religious traditions, beliefs, symbols, and rituals that reflect the religious dimension of an otherwise secular society.

**Civil Rights movement** the political protest movement of AFRICAN-AMERICANS against prevailing segregationist and discriminatory policies and traditions of white-dominated society. It sought the full participation of African-Americans in the political process and their full enjoyment of all rights guaranteed by the CONSTITUTION. Its high point was the March on WASHINGTON, D.C., led by MARTIN LUTHER KING, JR. in 1963.

**Civil War** the war between the 11 Southern slave states (the CONFEDERACY) and the UNION, fought between 1861 and 1865. Also called War Between the States, and War of Secession.

**clambake** a seashore picnic where clams and other foods are baked on hot stones in a hole in the ground, popular on the east coast of the United States.

**Clanton gang** See O.K. CORRAL.

**Clermont** the first commercially successful steamboat, built by ROBERT FULTON. It made its maiden voyage from New York City to Albany in 1807.

**Cleveland, Grover** 1837–1908. Twenty-second and twenty-fourth president of the United States (1885–1889 and 1893–1897).

**Clinton, Bill** 1946–. Forty-second president of the United States (1993–) and former governor of ARKANSAS.

**Clio** an annual award presented for excellence in the production of television commercials.

**cliometrics** historical study based on computer analysis of statistical data obtained from censuses and other sources.

**clockwork orange** depersonalized behavior induced by brainwashing or emotional conditioning by which human beings are trained to act like robots. (From the title of a 1962 novel by English author Anthony Burgess.)

**closet** hidden or unacknowledged in public, as in closet homosexual.

**cloverleaf intersection** a highway intersection with ramps that is shaped like a four-leaf clover, allowing the smooth flow of traffic in four directions.

**club sandwich** a popular sandwich made of three pieces of bread or toast with meat (usually bacon, turkey, ham, or chicken), lettuce, tomatoes, and mayonnaise in between.

**CO** COLORADO. (The official two-letter post office abbreviation.)

**coattail** the pull of a strong presidential candidate that helps to lift the electoral fortunes of lesser state and local political candidates.

**Coca-Cola** the trademarked name for a popular soft drink invented in 1886 by Atlanta pharmacist John S. Pemberton. Also known as *Coke*.

**cocooning** the avoidance of social contacts by persons preferring to spend leisure time in the privacy of the home. Coined by Faith Popcorn, social scientist.

**codependency** overreliance on persons, products, or chemical drugs, resulting from an inner instability and lack of self-reliance.

**coffee-table book** an oversized, lavishly illustrated, and expensive book designed not so much to be read as to be placed as an ornament on drawing room coffee tables.

**Coke** COCA-COLA.

**COLA** cost-of-living adjustment. A change in wages or SOCIAL SECURITY benefits determined by changes in the basic cost of living—a figure determined by the U.S. federal government.

**cold cut** a slice of cold meat. Cold cuts are often used in sandwiches. See also LUNCH MEAT.

**cold war** the intense military and political rivalry between the Soviet Union and Communist bloc nations on the one hand and the United States and its Western allies on the other. It lasted for over 35 years, from after WORLD WAR II to 1990.

**Cole, Thomas** 1801–1848. Painter. Cole was the first important landscape painter in America and the founder of the HUDSON RIVER SCHOOL of landscape painters.

**color man** a radio or television announcer who adds color to a broadcast by providing interesting sidelights and quips.

**Colorado** a state in the western United States in the ROCKY MOUNTAINS. Known as the Centennial State, its capital and largest city is Denver. Colorado's state bird is the lark bunting and its state flower is the Rocky Mountain columbine. Abbreviated CO.

**Colorado River** a river that rises in COLORADO and flows southwest to Mexico. It passes through the GRAND CANYON and contains HOOVER DAM.

**Columbia University** a university founded in 1754 as King's College and located in New York City. It is part of the IVY LEAGUE.

**Comanche** a Plains Indian people who occupied the region of TEXAS and OKLAHOMA in the 19th century. Warlike nomads and skillful equestrians, they were famous for their sun dances.

**Common Cause** a watchdog group founded in 1970 to campaign for political reform and for increased accountability and sensitivity of governmental leadership.

**commonwealth** the constitutional status of any one of four states in the United States: VIRGINIA, MASSACHUSETTS, KENTUCKY, and PENNSYLVANIA.

**Company, The** the CENTRAL INTELLIGENCE AGENCY (CIA).

**computer graphics** design or art generated through computer programs.

**computeracy** the ability to use computers and to perform basic tasks on them.

**Comsat** Communications Satellite, an artificial Earth satellite that transmits or relays electronic signals from any point on earth to any other point.

**Comstock, Anthony** See COMSTOCKERY.

**Comstock lode** the largest silver deposit ever found, located in the Nevada Mountains by prospector Henry Comstock in 1859.

**Comstockery** a derisory term coined by George Bernard Shaw to describe any puritanical campaign against pornography. From Anthony Comstock (1844–1915), secretary of the New York Society for the Suppression of Vice, who spearheaded a crusade against smutty mail in the 1870s.

**concrete poem** a form of nontraditional poetry in which words are arranged to form shapes and patterns in such a way that the entire poem appears as a drawing.

**Conestoga** a large horse-drawn wagon popular in the United States from the early 18th to the early 19th century. Named for the PENNSYLVANIA town where the covered wagons were built.

*Conestoga*

**Coney Island**  a resort and beach area on the Atlantic Ocean in Brooklyn (New York City).

**Confederacy**  the popular name for the Confederate States of America, which separated from the Union from 1861 to 1865. The original Confederate states were ALABAMA, GEORGIA, FLORIDA, LOUISIANA, MISSISSIPPI, and SOUTH CAROLINA. They were joined later by TEXAS, ARKANSAS, NORTH CAROLINA, TENNESSEE, and VIRGINIA.

**Confederate**  1. of or pertaining to the CONFEDERACY. 2. a supporter of the CONFEDERACY, especially a member of its army.

**conference call**  a telephone conference in which a central switching unit links a group of people. Also called *party call*.

**conglomerator**  the founder or chief executive officer of a conglomerate business enterprise.

**Congress**  the legislative branch of the U.S. government, consisting of the SENATE and the HOUSE OF REPRESENTATIVES. Both houses of Congress must pass a bill before it goes on to the president. The powers of Congress are set out in the CONSTITUTION.

**Connecticut**  a state in the northeastern United States. Called the Nutmeg State, its capital is Hartford and its largest city is Bridgeport. Connecticut's state flower is the mountain laurel and its state bird is the American robin. Abbreviated CT.

**Connecticut Yankee**  a crafty and ingenious YANKEE as depicted by MARK TWAIN in his *A Connecticut Yankee in King Arthur's Court*.

**conspicuous consumption**  the ostentatious display of luxuries as a means of establishing or enhancing one's status in society. Originally coined by THORSTEIN VEBLEN.

**Constitution**  the fundamental law of the United States. It was drafted in 1787 and became effective in 1789, replacing the ARTICLES OF CONFEDERATION. It consists of a preamble, seven articles, the BILL OF RIGHTS, and amendments. The Consitution sets up CONGRESS and describes its powers; creates the executive branch headed by the president; defines the country's legal system; provides for the separation of the legislative, judicial, and executive branches, ensuring that no one branch accumulates too much power; outlines the relationship between the states and the federal government; and provides for amendments to the document. The SUPREME COURT interprets the Constitution.

**Constitutional Convention** the 1787 meeting of delegates that resulted in the drafting of the CONSTITUTION. GEORGE WASHINGTON presided over the convention.

**consumer price index** an economic gauge of inflation that measures the average change in prices of basic goods and services over a particular period of time. Abbreviated CPI.

**consumerism** an economic philosophy that focuses on consumer rights, especially in such areas as product safety, fair pricing, and good workmanship.

**continental** worthless paper money issued by the CONTINENTAL CONGRESS during the REVOLUTIONARY WAR.

**Continental Congress** the legislature of the original THIRTEEN COLONIES that governed during the REVOLUTIONARY WAR and under the ARTICLES OF CONFEDERATION. The Congress first met in 1774 to discuss grievances against the British and adopted the DECLARATION OF INDEPENDENCE in 1776.

**contrarian** a stock broker who bucks popular trends and follows his nose in selecting investment stocks and bonds.

**controlled substance** a behavior-modifying substance whose production and sale are regulated by law.

**convenience store** a small store that is open long hours.

**conventional wisdom** commonly held beliefs subscribed to by the majority of the people and accepted without questioning.

**Conwell, Russell H.** See ACRES OF DIAMONDS.

**Coolidge, Calvin** 1872–1933. Thirtieth president of the United States (1923–1929).

**Cooper, Gary** 1901–1961. Actor. Cooper became a folk hero for his strong masculinity, laconic talk, and commanding and rugged presence. He won an ACADEMY AWARD for his performance in *High Noon* (1952).

**Cooper, James Fenimore** 1789–1851. Novelist. The first American popular novelist, he wrote the *Leatherstocking Tales*, a collection of novels about the early frontier, which included *The Pioneers* (1823), *The Last of the Mohicans* (1826), and *The Deerslayer* (1841).

**Cooper, Peter** 1791–1883. Industrialist and philanthropist. An industrialist with strong holdings in glue, iron, and telegraph, Cooper was one of the earliest socially conscious businessmen in America and helped to found the Cooper Union for Advancement of Science and Art, a free school, in New York City.

**Copland, Aaron** 1900–1990. Composer. Copland created a truly American 20th-century musical language marked by complex rhythms and dissonant harmonies.

**Copley, John Singleton** 1738–1815. Painter. Copley is regarded as the first great American portraitist.

**copperhead** a Northern sympathizer of the CONFEDERATE cause during the CIVIL WAR, from the poisonous snake of the same name.

**copreneurship** a husband-and-wife business partnership.

**copyright** the exclusive right to publish, produce, and sell a print or electronic work granted by law to its author or his or her publisher for a specified number of years.

**core city** See CENTRAL CITY.

**Corn Belt** a region in the MIDWEST, consisting of ILLINOIS, INDIANA, IOWA, and MISSOURI, where the soil and climate are well suited for growing corn.

**corn pone** a simple bread made with cornmeal, popular in the SOUTH. *Pone* is from ALGONQUIN.

**cornbread** bread made with cornmeal.

**Cornell University** an IVY LEAGUE university in NEW YORK that was chartered in 1865. It was named for its founder, businessman Ezra Cornell (1807–1874).

**Cornhusker State** Nebraska.

**cornmeal mush** a soft food made by boiling cornmeal in water or milk. It is usually formed into loaves, sliced, and fried.

**cornpone** a corny kind of folksy humor, supposedly typical of the South.

**correctional facility** a politically correct euphemism for a prison.

**Cosa Nostra** the code name for the Mafia. From Italian for "our thing."

**Cotton Belt** a region of the United States where the main agricultural crop was cotton. The term usually includes the states of Alabama, Arkansas, Georgia, Louisiana, Mississippi, North Carolina, Oklahoma, South Carolina, and Texas, and parts of Florida, Kentucky, Missouri, and Tennessee.

**cotton candy** a confection made from colored sugar that is spun until it resembles cotton and then wrapped around a paper cone or a stick.

**cotton gin** a machine that separates cotton fiber from the seeds. Invented by Eli Whitney in 1793, it revolutionized the processing of cotton.

**couch potato** a person who spends a great deal of time watching television.

*children eating cotton candy*

**cougar** a mountain lion.

**counterculture** an antiestablishment lifestyle espoused by the New Left, hippies, Black Panthers and others opposed to mainstream society. Its catchphrases were *Do your own thing* and *Tune in, turn on, and drop out.*

**country music**  distinctively American music combining many elements, such as mountain or hillbilly music, ballads, GOSPEL, BLUES, and folk tunes of the Southwest. The last is so influential that country music is sometimes called Country and Western. The characteristic themes of country music are homesickness, wanderlust, failed romance, and death. The home of country music is Nashville, TENNESSEE, where the GRAND OLE OPRY is its most celebrated showcase.

**county**  the political and geographical subdivision of each state except LOUISIANA, where this unit is called a PARISH.

**county seat**  the town or city that contains the government and administrative offices of a COUNTY.

**coverage**  shots, including close-ups and reverse angles, that a film director takes in addition to the master shot.

**covered bridge**  a typical enclosed rural bridge constructed of wood found in NEW ENGLAND and parts of the MIDWEST.

**covered wagon**  a wagon drawn by oxen, mules, or horses and covered with a tentlike canvas tarpaulin. Originally made in CONESTOGA, PENNSYLVANIA, it was used to carry passengers and freight in the 19th century. The wagons would form circles whenever threatened with attacks from NATIVE AMERICANS. (Also called a *prairie schooner.*)

**covert action**  clandestine activities carried on by a national intelligence-gathering organization, such as the CIA.

**cowboy**  a skilled horseman whose duties include herding and branding cattle. In the OLD WEST, cowboys often drove cattle great distances to pasture. Nowadays, most cowboys work on fenced ranches. Cowboys have been glorified in WESTERNS, where they are often depicted as violent Indian killers.

**cowpoke**  a COWBOY.

**cowpuncher**  a COWBOY.

**Coyote State**  SOUTH DAKOTA.

**CPA**  CERTIFIED PUBLIC ACCOUNTANT.

**CPI** CONSUMER PRICE INDEX.

**cracker** 1. a thin and crispy biscuit, often served as a snack with cheese. 2. a poor, white person living in the southeast United States (derogatory).

**Cradle of Liberty** the nickname of FANEUIL HALL, the Boston town hall where early anti-British meetings were held.

**Cram, Ralph Adams** 1863–1942. Architect. He is best known for his Gothic Revival buildings at the U.S. Military Academy and PRINCETON UNIVERSITY, and the Cathedral of St. John the Divine in New York City.

**cranberry** a tart, bright red berry that grows in bogs. Cranberry sauce is a traditional THANKSGIVING dinner dish.

**Crane, Stephen** 1871–1900. Novelist and war correspondent. Scion of an old Colonial family, Crane is best known for *The Red Badge of Courage* (1895), one of the finest CIVIL WAR novels ever written.

**craps** a popular dice game in which players roll two dice in hopes of getting a winning 7 or 11.

**cream cheese** a soft white cheese made either partially or wholly from cream.

**cremains** the ashes of a cremated corpse.

**Creole** 1. a person of French or Spanish descent in old LOUISIANA. Creole culture is distinguished by its rich cuisine as well as its aristocratic customs. Sometimes, the term is extended to persons of mixed Spanish or French and African-American descent. 2. the French dialect spoken by LOUISIANA Creoles.

**critical mass** the level at which a certain desirable goal is achieved, especially when the number or amount of contributory agents reaches the required minimum.

**crossover** the act of crossing the boundaries between two styles or modes, especially in music.

**cruise control** a computer-controlled mechanism that enables a driver to set the speed of an automobile on a highway.

**CST** CENTRAL STANDARD TIME.

**CT** CONNECTICUT. (The official two-letter post office abbreviation.)

**cult figure** the central figure in a cult or the object of adulation among cult members.

**culture shock** initial feelings of disorientation and confusion on encountering an alien society and the accompanying difficulty in readjusting one's social norms and values.

**Cumberland Gap** a natural pass in the APPALACHIAN MOUNTAINS where the borders of KENTUCKY, VIRGINIA, and TENNESSEE meet.

**cummings, e. e.** 1894–1962. Poet. Cummings is known for his inventive use of language and typography.

**Currier and Ives** a printmaking firm founded by Nathaniel Currier (1813–1888). In 1853 artist James Merritt Ives (1824–1895) was made a partner. The firm was known for its hand-colored lithographs illustrating 19th-century daily life.

**Currier, Nathaniel** See CURRIER AND IVES.

**cursor** the flashing symbol on a computer display screen that shows the place where the next insertion will appear.

**curtain raiser** a short act before the main performance.

**Custer, George Armstrong** See LITTLE BIGHORN, BATTLE OF THE.

**Custer's Last Stand** LITTLE BIGHORN, BATTLE OF THE.

**cutaway** a brief shot that interrupts the continuity of a main action of a film, often used to show concurrent events.

**cutting edge** the dynamic forefront where the most innovative breakthroughs occur and where the best ideas are concentrated.

**Dakota** a NATIVE AMERICAN people, also known as the SIOUX, who live in NORTH DAKOTA, SOUTH DAKOTA, and parts of MINNESOTA and MONTANA.

**Dakotas** the states of NORTH DAKOTA and SOUTH DAKOTA.

**Dana, Charles Anderson** 1819–1897. Editor. As the editor of two great New York newspapers, Dana was a powerful influence on the UNION side in the CIVIL WAR.

**Dana, Richard Henry, Jr.** 1815–1882. Author. Best known for the classic sea tale *Two Years Before the Mast* (1840), Dana was also an active reformer and lawyer.

**Danforth** to advise a patient at the time of admission to a hospital of his or her right to refuse life-sustaining measures if necessary. From John Danforth, former U.S. Senator who sponsored legislation requiring such a right.

**DAR** DAUGHTERS OF THE AMERICAN REVOLUTION.

**Dare, Virginia** born in 1587, Dare was the first English child born in the NEW WORLD. Her parents were Eleanor and Ananias Dare, settlers in JAMESTOWN Colony.

**Darrow, Clarence** 1857–1938. Lawyer. Darrow was a defender of unpopular causes whose most famous client was John L. Scopes, the TENNESSEE teacher whom he defended in the famous SCOPES TRIAL (1925).

**Dartmouth College** an IVY LEAGUE university located in Hanover, NEW HAMPSHIRE. Dartmouth opened in 1770 and emphasizes liberal arts.

**database** a collection of computerized data or records that may be retrieved at will or reorganized in any desired order.

**Daughters of the American Revolution** a conservative patriotic organization, founded in 1890, whose members trace their lineage to the REVOLUTIONARY WAR period. Abbreviated DAR.

**Davis, Bette** 1908–1989. Actress. Davis portrayed a wide variety of characters, from heroines to eccentrics to wicked women, with a unique intensity. She won two ACADEMY AWARDS for Best Actress for her work in *Dangerous* (1935) and *Jezebel* (1938).

**dawk** a blend of a DOVE and a HAWK, a person who is more belligerent than a dove and more conciliatory than a hawk.

**Day, Dorothy** 1897–1980. Catholic social reformer, founder of the Catholic Worker Movement. A devout Roman Catholic as well as a fervent but nonviolent social radical, Day helped to open Catholic thinking to concepts of social justice.

**daylight saving time** a system, authorized by CONGRESS, by which time is advanced by one hour between the first Sunday in April and the last Sunday in October, providing an extra hour of light in the evening. Abbreviated DST.

**DC** DISTRICT OF COLUMBIA. (The official two-letter post office abbreviation.)

**de Kooning, Willem** 1904–1997. Painter. De Kooning was born in The Netherlands and came to the United States as a stowaway. He was a major figure in the New York school of abstract expressionism of the 1940s.

**de Mille, Agnes George** 1909–1993. Choreographer and dancer. Her dance narratives changed forever the relationship between the ballet and the BROADWAY musical.

**DE** DELAWARE. (The official two-letter post office abbreviation.)

**Deadheads** fans of the musical group the Grateful Dead, a pioneer ACID ROCK band in the 1960s.

**Dean, James** 1931–1955. Actor. An intense actor who usually played the role of a troubled youth, Dean starred in only three movies before his death in a car accident at the age of twenty-four. Dean remains a popular American cult figure today.

**Death Valley** a desert basin 282 feet below sea level in southern CALIFORNIA containing the lowest point in the Western Hemisphere.

*James Dean*

**debit card** a card that enables a person to purchase goods and services by charging them directly against funds on deposit at a bank.

**Debs, Eugene** 1855–1926. Socialist labor leader. A veteran union organizer, Debs cofounded the INDUSTRIAL WORKERS OF THE WORLD and was the presidential candidate for the Socialist Party between 1900 and 1921.

**Declaration of Independence** the founding document of the United States, proclaiming the severance of ties with the British monarchy, issued on July 4, 1776.

**Decoration Day** See MEMORIAL DAY.

**decriminalize** to remove a former crime from the criminal code and to make its commission nonpunishable.

**dedicated** set apart for a specific task or designed for a special purpose.

**deep pockets** immensely rich, with seemingly limitless financial resources.

## Deep South

**Deep South** the region covering GEORGIA, ALABAMA, MISSISSIPPI and LOUISIANA.

**deep think** a pedantic analysis of a problem that appears profound without being really so.

**Delaware** 1. a NATIVE AMERICAN people, known as Leni Lenape, who lived in the 18th century in an area that is now covered by NEW JERSEY, NEW YORK, and DELAWARE. 2. a state in the eastern United States. Called the Diamond State or the First State, Delaware's capital is Dover and its largest city is Wilmington. The bluehen chicken is Delaware's state bird and the peach blossom is its state flower.

**Delphi** a method of forecasting future trends by assembling and analyzing the answers of a group of experts to a series of carefully posed questions.

**Delta blues** a type of BLUES music influenced by COUNTRY MUSIC.

**demand-side** of or relating to an economic policy that stimulates demand for goods and services as a means of spurring the economy and increasing employment. Compare SUPPLY-SIDE. Also called Keynesianism.

**DeMille, Cecil B.** 1881–1959. Film director and producer. One of HOLLYWOOD's first filmmakers, he was an unparalleled showman who specialized in colossal epics.

**Democratic Party** a political party, generally associated with left-of-center or liberal policies, founded in 1791 as the Jeffersonian Republican Party. It was the party of the slave states in the CIVIL WAR. Its symbol is the donkey.

**demographics** statistics dealing with the size, distribution, and economic status of the population.

**demonize** to portray a person or group as evil by exaggerating its real or imaginary harmful actions or characteristics.

**Department of Defense** the executive department of the U.S. government in charge of the military forces for war and security. Abbreviated DOD.

**Department of Energy** the executive department of the U.S. government in charge of the administration of the nation's energy policies, including research and development, conservation, regulation, and nuclear arms. Abbreviated DOE.

**Department of Health and Human Services** the executive department of the U.S. government in charge of public health and welfare policies. Abbreviated as HHS, it includes the SOCIAL SECURITY ADMINISTRATION and the PUBLIC HEALTH SERVICE.

**Department of Public Health** a state or municipal agency that administers the health care system of its jurisdiction. Abbreviated DPH.

**Department of State** the executive department of the U.S. government reponsible for the conduct of U.S. foreign policy. Commonly called the State Department, it negotiates treaties with foreign nations, represents the United States at international conferences, and issues passports and visas. Sometimes referred to as the *Foggy Bottom*.

**deprogram** to pull back a person from the grip of a cult or sect by exposing its harmful teachings and by offering alternative psychological or monetary inducements.

**Desert Storm** the PERSIAN GULF WAR.

**designer drug** a drug altered by chemists or pharmacists so that it does not fall under the category of illegal controlled substances.

**Dewey decimal system** the standard library book cataloging system devised by librarian Melvil Dewey (1851–1931).

**Dewey, John** 1859–1952. Educator and philosopher. A seminal thinker who left an indelible imprint on American ideas on education and philosophy, Dewey was the prime exponent of Pragmatism, which he used as a basis for social reform.

**Dewey, Melvil** See DEWEY DECIMAL SYSTEM.

**Diamond State** DELAWARE.

**Dickinson, Emily** 1830–1886. Poet. Considered America's first great woman poet, Dickinson created subtle lyric poems of great range and intensity. Her poems, nearly 2,000 in all, were published posthumously.

**digerati** the experts and specialists of the information society.

**dime novel** a book of romantic or sensational popular fiction published in paperback and priced at ten cents, popular between 1860 and 1900. Also known as a YELLOWBACK.

**dinner theater** a restaurant where dinner is followed by a theatrical production, with a combined price for both.

*Emily Dickinson*

**disc jockey** one who plays recorded music on the radio or for public dancing.

**discipling** in certain Pentecostal churches, the practice of creating small cells of believers, each under the authority of a mature leader who is expected to shepherd the spiritual growth of all members of the cell.

**disco** dance music whose popularity soared in the late 1970s, characterized by a repetitive beat, often featuring synthesizers instead of instruments.

**discouraged worker** an unemployed worker who leaves the employment market after failing to find an appropriate job despite efforts.

**disinformation** false information presented as true to mislead people or to influence them to act in a certain manner.

**Disney, Walt** 1901–1966. Cartoon animator and film producer. Disney founded a vast entertainment conglomerate with interests in movies, THEME PARKS, and music. His most popular animated character, MICKEY MOUSE, was introduced in a 1928 cartoon.

**Disneyland**  the trademarked name of a THEME PARK in Anaheim, CALIFORNIA, created by WALT DISNEY that opened in 1955. It is a major tourist attraction.

**diss**  to treat disrespectfully.

**dissolve**  in film, the gradual transformation of one scene into the next by merging a fade-out with a fade-in.

**distance education**  educational programs on radio, television, and the INTERNET.

**District of Columbia**  the district of the United States occupied by WASHINGTON, D.C., the country's capital. Abbreviated DC.

**Dixie**  1. term for the SOUTH, probably derived from the MASON-DIXON LINE. 2. a song composed by northerner Daniel Decatur Emmett that was very popular in the SOUTH during the CIVIL WAR.

**Dixiecrat**  a southern Democrat who opposed the civil rights plank of the DEMOCRATIC PARTY from the time of HARRY S. TRUMAN.

**Dixieland**  a form of JAZZ music characterized by fast rhythms and brass instruments. It originated in New Orleans, LOUISIANA, in the early 1900s.

**DJIA**  DOW-JONES INDUSTRIAL AVERAGE.

**DOA**  1. dead on arrival, said of persons who are pronounced dead when they reach a hospital emergency room. 2. any idea or program that is lifeless at inception.

**DOB**  date of birth. (Commonly found on forms.)

**docudrama**  a television dramatization based on real events or persons.

**docutainment**  a television program based on documentary material.

**DOD**  DEPARTMENT OF DEFENSE.

**Dodge City**  KANSAS railhead that gained notoriety in the 1880s as the "wickedest little city in America."

**DOE**  DEPARTMENT OF ENERGY.

**Doe, Jane**  See JOHN DOE; JANE DOE.

**Doe, John**  See JOHN DOE; JANE DOE.

**doggie bag**  a bag or container provided by a restaurant to a diner upon request so that he or she can take leftover food home, supposedly for the family pet.

**dolly shot**  in film, a moving shot taken from a wheeled camera platform known as a dolly.

**domino effect**  a chain reaction in which a series of objects is so positioned that the fall of one brings down its neighbor.

**donkey**  symbol of the DEMOCRATIC PARTY, first drawn by THOMAS NAST in a cartoon.

**doo-wop**  a 1950s style of music in which nonsense syllables are sung in unison by small groups.

**Dos Passos, John Roderigo**  1896–1970. Novelist. He is best known for his trilogy *U.S.A.* (1938), which follows the rise of materialism in America from the late 19th century to the GREAT DEPRESSION.

**double pumping**  presenting the same program twice in one night or twice in one week as a means of reinforcing audience interest.

**Doubleday, Abner**  See BASEBALL.

**doubleheader**  two sporting events played back-to-back. It is more common in BASEBALL than in other sports.

**doughboy**  an American GI in WORLD WAR I.

**Douglass, Frederick**  1817–1895. Black editor, orator, and abolitionist. Douglass was the most influential AFRICAN-AMERICAN leader of the 19th century. A slave born to a black mother and white father, Douglass gained national attention in 1841 as a protégé of WILLIAM LLOYD

*Frederick Douglass*

GARRISON and as an orator in abolitionist meetings. He wrote the first major African-American autobiography and published a widely read abolitionist newspaper, *The North Star*.

**dove** a person who favors a lower U.S. military profile and disengagement from military actions abroad.

**Dow, Charles H.** See DOW-JONES INDUSTRIAL AVERAGE.

**Dow-Jones Industrial Average** an index of the stock price performance of 30 well-known and well-run companies. It is used as an overall indication of the strength of the stock market, originally devised by economists Charles H. Dow and Edward D. Jones. Often referred to as The Dow and abbreviated DJIA.

**Down East** term for NEW ENGLAND in general and MAINE in particular. So called because vessels sailing to Maine would be sailing east down the prevailing winds.

**downsize** to reduce in size. By extension, to make a corporation more profitable, efficient, and wieldy by reducing the workforce.

**downstream** the phase of industrial operation dealing with the later stages of distribution and marketing. Compare UPSTREAM.

**downtown** the main section of a city; the part of a city in which major businesses are located.

**DPH** DEPARTMENT OF PUBLIC HEALTH.

**Dr. Death** DR. JACK KEVORKIAN.

**Dr. Feelgood** a physician or counselor who focuses on making the patient psychologically happy rather than curing diseases or addressing problems.

**Dr. Pepper** a trademarked brand of soft drink created in 1885 in Wade Morrison's Waco, TEXAS, drugstore.

**dream team** an ideal group of specialists or athletes enlisted to perform a special task.

**Dreiser, Theodore** 1871–1945. Novelist. Dreiser's controversial and unconventional novels shocked puritan readers with their portrayals of real-life tragedies caused by greed and inhumanity. His works include *Sister Carrie* (1900) and *An American Tragedy* (1925).

**drop**  a large painted fabric used as scenery on a stage.

**DST**  DAYLIGHT SAVING TIME.

**Du Bois, W. E. B.**  1868–1963. Civil rights leader and scholar. Called the Father of Pan-Africanism, Du Bois represented the crest of a black renaissance movement. He combined his ideological crusades with his skills as a scholar to promote AFRICAN-AMERICAN perspectives. In his quest for full civil and political rights for blacks, Du Bois cofounded the National Association for the Advancement of Colored People (NAACP) in 1910.

**dude**  a person from the city, especially a tourist at a DUDE RANCH.

**dude ranch**  a place catering to DUDES or COWBOYS; a ranch for vacationing city people.

**DUI**  driving under the influence. The charge applied to people arrested for driving while drunk. Compare with DWI.

**Duncan, Isadora**  1878–1927. Dancer. A pioneer in the modern dance movement, she helped to liberate both ballet and its performers from the bonds of convention.

**dune buggy**  a small, lightweight car designed for driving on beaches and sand dunes.

**Durand, Asher B.**  1796–1886. Painter. Durand led the HUDSON RIVER SCHOOL along with THOMAS COLE.

**dust bowl**  the GREAT PLAINS from TEXAS to the DAKOTAS, scene of one of the worst droughts in American history in the 1930s.

*dune buggy*

**DWEM**  Dead White European Male, a reference to the Caucasian males who have dominated Western Civilization.

**DWI** driving while intoxicated. The charge applied to people arrested for driving while drunk. Called DUI in some areas.

**Dylan, Bob** 1941–. Singer and one of the most influential songwriters of the 1960s. Born Robert Zimmerman, he spearheaded the FOLK REVIVAL and wrote protest songs that had a seminal influence on other musicians of his era.

**dystopia** a place or condition that is difficult or diseased or characterized by conflict and unhappiness; the opposite of utopia.

# E

*e pluribus unum* the motto on the Great Seal of the United States. It is Latin for *out of many, one.*

**Eakins, Thomas** 1844–1916. Painter. Eakins specialized in the human figure and is most famous for portraits. His realism shocked his contemporaries but left an impact on the AshCAN School.

**Eames, Charles** 1907–1978. Architect and furniture designer. His innovative designs, particularly the Eames chair, helped to institute an authentic American style in furniture.

**Earhart, Amelia** 1898–1937. Pioneering aviator. In 1932, Earhart became the first woman to fly solo across the Atlantic Ocean. In 1935, she flew across the Pacific Ocean from Honolulu, Hawaii to California. Her attempt to fly around the world ended in tragedy as her plane disappeared over the Pacific Ocean in 1937.

**Earp, Wyatt** 1848–1929. Lawman and gunfighter. Wyatt, along with his three brothers, Virgil, Morgan, and James, was involved in the famous shootout at the O.K. Corral against the Clanton gang, a group of suspected cattle rustlers.

*Amelia Earhart*

**Earth Day** a day in April set aside unofficially to mark concern for the Earth and environment and for activities designed to promote awareness of ecological problems.

**eastern daylight time** the adjusted time in the eastern United States during early April to late October. It is four hours behind Greenwich time. Abbreviated EDT.

**eastern standard time** the time in the eastern quarter of the United States from the last weekend in October to the first weekend in April. It is five hours behind Greenwich time. Abbreviated EST.

**Eastman, George** 1854–1932. Inventor. Eastman revolutionized photography with his Kodak box camera and flexible roll film.

**Ebonics** Black vernacular English, especially the peculiarities of syntax, grammar, and pronunciation that distinguish AFRICAN-AMERICAN speech from standard English.

**economic crime** any of a number of criminal offenses against economic regulations, such as money laundering, insider trading and black marketeering.

**Eddy, Mary Baker** 1821–1910. Founder of CHRISTIAN SCIENCE, a denomination that began as an association devoted to physical healing through prayer.

**edge city** an urban community that develops on the outskirts of a large city but is more autonomous than a suburb.

**Edison, Thomas Alva** 1847–1931. Inventor. The foremost American inventor, he is credited with a host of inventions, including the motion picture (the Vitascope), light bulb and light socket, electricity generating plant, telegraph, dynamo, storage battery, dictaphone, mimeograph, microphone, electric locomotive, and signaling devices.

**Edsel** 1. Ford automobile introduced in 1957, named after Edsel Ford, son of HENRY FORD. Its garish design made it one of the worst-selling automobiles in history. 2. any notable failure.

**EDT** EASTERN DAYLIGHT TIME.

**Edwards, Jonathan** 1703–1758. Religious leader. The Prince of Puritans, Edwards was an incomparable although austere theologian who emphasized God's judgment rather than His mercy. He helped to spark the nation's first religious revival known as the GREAT AWAKENING.

**EEOC** EQUAL EMPLOYMENT OPPORTUNITY COMMISSION.

**EFT** ELECTRONIC FUNDS TRANSFER.

**egghead** an intellectual (informal).

**ego trip** anything done solely to boost one's ego or indulge one's appetites.

**800 number** a telephone number with an AREA CODE of 800. There is no charge for calling an 800 number.

**18-wheeler** a truck with eighteen wheels on five axles.

**Einstein, Albert** 1879–1955. Physicist. A giant among modern scientists, Einstein devised the theory of relativity, which revolutionized physics and cosmology.

**Eisenhower, Dwight David** 1890–1969. Thirty-fourth president of the United States (1953–1961). He was the supreme commander of the Allied troops during WORLD WAR II.

**ekistics** the study of the formation and evolution of human settlements, particularly towns and cities.

**Electoral College** the body of electors established by the U.S. CONSTITUTION to elect the president. Each state is represented in the Electoral College by a set number of electors.

**electronic church** a religious service or mass, conducted on television or radio by dynamic preachers and serving to substitute or supplement worship or healing services in a local church.

**electronic funds transfer** a bank-directed transfer of funds from one account to another by computer. Commonly abbreviated as EFT.

**electronic journalism** See BROADCAST JOURNALISM.

**electronic publishing** publishing in nonprint formats, such as on-line, tapes, optical disks, or CD-ROMs.

**electronic warfare** warfare conducted through electronic devices, such as interruption of enemy warheads through computer-directed missiles.

**elephant** symbol of the REPUBLICAN PARTY, first drawn by THOMAS NAST in a cartoon.

**el(evated train)** a train that travels on tracks that are elevated, enabling pedestrian and other traffic to travel below. Most often seen in large cities.

**elevator** a mechanical device that carries people from floor to floor in a building.

**elevator music** soft, mild background music. Also called MUZAK.

**Eliot, Charles William** 1834–1926. Educator. President of HARVARD UNIVERSITY (1869–1919), Eliot transformed it into the institution it is today. He reorganized it as a college of undergraduate studies surrounded by autonomous graduate and professional schools, increased faculty salaries and the number of faculty members, instituted sabbaticals, and improved the quality and methods of instruction. He also edited the HARVARD CLASSICS.

**Eliot, John** 1604–1690. English-born preacher who was the first to preach to Native Americans in their own language. The first Bible published in North America was one translated by him into ALGONQUIAN.

**Eliot, T. S.** 1888–1965. U.S.-born British poet whose heavily allusive poems, particularly *The Waste Land*, helped him to win the Nobel Prize for Literature in 1948.

**Elks** social organization founded in 1868, originally only for white male citizens of the United States. Its member lodges are active in philanthropy. Its full name is the Benevolent and Protective Order of Elks.

**Ellington, Duke** 1899–1974. Composer and JAZZ pianist. He created the Ellington sound, a distinctive sound that defied replication. Among his masterpieces were "Mood Indigo" (1931) and "Sophisticated Lady" (1933).

**Ellis Island** a set of small connected islands in New York Bay which, during the latter part of the 19th century and the early part of the 20th century, was the entry point for millions of foreign immigrants, especially from Europe.

**Ellison, Ralph Waldo** 1914–1994. AFRICAN-AMERICAN author. Ellison's novel *Invisible Man* (1952), detailing society's treatment of African-Americans, is considered a classic of American literature.

**e-mail** electronic mail transmitted over the INTERNET.

**Emanicipation Proclamation** President ABRAHAM LINCOLN's executive order of January 1, 1863, freeing all slaves in both UNION and CONFEDERATE states.

**Emerson, Ralph Waldo** 1803–1882. Essayist, philosopher. Known as the Sage of Concord, he was one of the most influential writers and thinkers of the 19th century and leader of the philosophical movement known as TRANSCENDENTALISM. Despite being a liberal, Emerson spoke out against the dry-as-dust rationalism of his day as well as against religious orthodoxy, favoring, instead, individual intuitive experience.

**Emmy Awards** awards for outstanding television performances given annually since 1949 by the National Academy of Television Arts and Sciences.

**emoticon** symbol used to indicate emotions, such as humor or irony, in electronic messages. Also called *smiley*.

**Empire State** the state of NEW YORK.

**Empire State Building** located in New York City, it was the tallest building in the world from 1931 to 1972. With the television antennas, its height is 1,472 ft.

*Empire State Building*

**Employee Stock Ownership Plan** a system that encourages company employees to own company stock. Abbreviated ESOP.

**empty nest** a home where the children have grown up and left the parents alone.

**encryption** process by which information in alphabetical or numerical form is transformed or scrambled into a cipher or code that cannot be read without the help of a descrambler.

**engineered food** food treated chemically to enhance its flavor, increase its nutritional value or prolong its storage life.

**English muffin** a round, flat muffin that is first baked on a griddle and then is toasted and eaten for breakfast.

***Enola Gay*** The B-29 superfortress bomber that dropped the atomic bomb on Hiroshima, Japan, on August 6, 1945.

**enterprise zone** an urban area of high unemployment targeted for special government programs offering incentives, such as reduced taxes, for business enterprises.

**EPCOT Center** one of the three major parks that make up WALT DISNEY WORLD located near Orlando, FLORIDA. The acronym stands for Experimental Prototype Community of Tomorrow.

**Equal Employment Opportunity Commission** a government agency that handles discrimination complaints in employment situations. Abbreviated EEOC.

**equal opportunity** nondiscriminatory practices in hiring employees regardless of race, gender, age, religion, color, etc.

**Equal Rights Amendment** a proposed amendment to the U.S. CONSTITUTION, first introduced in 1923, outlawing discrimination based on gender. It has never been ratified. Abbreviated ERA.

**equal time** the legal right of a candidate for a public office to comparable time in the same media in order to respond to charges by his or her opponent.

**Equality State** WYOMING.

**ERA** 1. earned run average, a BASEBALL term. For every nine innings pitched, the average number of earned runs scored by batters against a particular pitcher. 2. EQUAL RIGHTS AMENDMENT.

**Erie Canal** a manmade canal completed in 1825 that connects the Hudson River and Lake Erie. The canal increased trade and contributed to the development of New York City and other large cities. Nicknamed the *Big Ditch*.

**ESL** English as a second language. Referring to the English language as taught to nonnative speakers.

**ESOP** EMPLOYEE STOCK OWNERSHIP PLAN.

**EST** EASTERN STANDARD TIME.

**establishment** the power structure of a nation or society consisting of the traditional and entrenched ruling elites or institutions.

**ethnic** a member of a cultural or racial minority. Generally, the term excludes white Anglo-Saxon Protestants, AFRICAN-AMERICANS, and NATIVE AMERICANS.

***Evangeline*** 1847 verse romance by HENRY WADSWORTH LONGFELLOW narrating the story of an Acadian couple, Gabriel Lajeunesse and Evangeline Bellefontane, who were separated when the British deported the Acadians to LOUISIANA in 1755 but were later reunited when they were old.

**Everglades** southern FLORIDA swamplands covering almost 5,000 square miles and containing a wide variety of plant and animal life.

**Evergreen State** WASHINGTON.

**exacta** a method of betting in horse racing in which the bettor not only picks the winning horses, but also places them in the exact order of the finish.

**exit poll** a poll of voters to find out for whom they voted, usually taken as they leave the polling booth.

**expressway** a highway that has no stops or intersections, designed for quick travel.

**FAA** Federal Aviation Administration.

**face-off** a confrontation between opponents.

**faction** a literary work that presents facts in the form of fiction or real people in the guise of fictional characters, often to escape legal penalties for libel.

**factoid** an unsubstantiated statement that is widely accepted as fact simply because it appears in print.

**failsafe** designed to prevent malfunction by mechanically stopping or modifying operation.

**fair use** a principle embodied in copyright law that permits use of portions of copyrighted materials without the sanction of the copyright owner provided the use is fair and reasonable, does not exceed 250 to 400 words in length, is for the purpose of advancing scholarship, and is accompanied by fair author attribution.

**Falwell, Jerry** 1933–. Evangelist. A conservative active both in politics and ministry, in the 1970s Falwell founded both Lynchburg Baptist College in Virginia and the Moral Majority.

**family values** the values that sustain an average nuclear family, especially moral imperatives, religious faith, familial care and devotion, respect for parents, etc.

**Faneuil Hall** Boston market and meeting hall built in Colonial times. Presented to the city in 1742 by merchant Peter Faneuil, it was a center of anti-British meetings before the Revolutionary War. Also called the *Cradle of Liberty*.

**Fannie Mae** nicknamed for FEDERAL NATIONAL MORTGAGE ASSOCIATION.

**FAQ** frequently asked questions in a news group on the INTERNET.

**fast food** standardized food prepared in assembly line procedures and dispensed without the help of waiters or waitresses.

**fast lane** a way of life characterized by fast pace and instant gratification.

**Father of His Country** GEORGE WASHINGTON.

**Father of Waters** MISSISSIPPI RIVER.

**Father's Day** national holiday honoring fathers, celebrated since 1927 on the third Sunday in June.

**Faulkner, William** 1897–1962. Novelist. Faulkner, a literary giant, won the Nobel Prize for Literature in 1949. Most of his novels are set in the SOUTH in mythical Yoknapatawpha County. *The Sound and the Fury* (1929) is an example of his mastery of fiction.

**favorite son** in a presidential nominating convention, a person nominated by his own party delegation. Favorite sons enjoy strong leverage in deadlocked conventions.

**FBI** FEDERAL BUREAU OF INVESTIGATION. Often called the *Fed*.

**FCC** FEDERAL COMMUNICATIONS COMMISSION.

**FDA** FOOD AND DRUG ADMINISTRATION.

**FDIC** FEDERAL DEPOSIT INSURANCE CORPORATION.

**FDR** FRANKLIN DELANO ROOSEVELT.

**Fed** 1. the federal government in general. 2. the FEDERAL BUREAU OF INVESTIGATION, or one of its agents. 3. the FEDERAL RESERVE SYSTEM.

**Federal Aviation Administration** an agency within the Department of Transportation that oversees policies regarding air traffic, airspace, and other aviation matters. Abbreviated FAA.

**Federal Bureau of Investigation** a division of the U.S. Department of Justice that investigates violations of federal laws. Commonly called the FBI.

**Federal Communications Commission** an agency that regulates telephone, television, radio, and satellite communications. Abbreviated FCC.

**Federal Deposit Insurance Corporation** an agency established in 1933 to insure deposits of state banks that do not belong to the Federal Reserve System. Abbreviated FDIC.

**Federal Housing Administration** a division within the Department of Housing and Urban Development that insures mortgages. Abbreviated FHA.

**Federal Insurance Contributions Act** the legislation that withholds money from income to go toward SOCIAL SECURITY. Its acronym, FICA, is found on paycheck stubs.

**Federal National Mortgage Association** a government lending agency that buys and sells federally insured mortgages. Abbreviated FNMA, it is often referred to as Fannie Mae.

**Federal Register** the official journal recording all transactions of the federal government, including executive orders and appointments.

**Federal Reserve Board** the policy-making body of the FEDERAL RESERVE SYSTEM. Abbreviated FRB.

**Federal Reserve System** the United States centralized banking system created to monitor the economy by regulating the money supply. Often called the *Fed*.

**Federal Savings and Loan Insurance Corporation** the government agency that insured the deposits of member savings and loan institutions until 1989, when it went broke. Abbreviated FSLIC.

**federal style** a neoclassical architectural style popularized at the turn of the 19th century by CHARLES BULFINCH and others. It was characterized by white columns against red brick walls and fanlight windows on doorways.

**Federal Trade Commission** a commission established in 1914 to promote competition and free enterprise by breaking up monopolies and to prevent trade restraints and unfair trading practices. Abbreviated FTC.

***Federalist, The*** a collection of essays published in 1777 and 1778 by "Publius," a collective pseudonym of ALEXANDER HAMILTON, JAMES MADISON, and JOHN JAY, urging the ratification of the U.S. CONSTITUTION. Also known as the *Federalist Papers.*

**Ferlinghetti, Lawrence** 1919–. Poet. A BEAT GENERATION poet, Ferlinghetti owned a San Francisco bookstore in the 1950s that was popular with BEATNIKS.

*Ferris wheel*

**Ferris wheel** an amusement park ride in which a large vertical wheel with evenly spaced passenger cars rotates on its axis. It was designed by George Washington Gale Ferris and first demonstrated at the 1893 Chicago World Columbian Exhibition.

**FHA** FEDERAL HOUSING ADMINISTRATION.

**fiber optics** a bundle of flexible glass or plastic filaments that can transmit light.

**FICA** FEDERAL INSURANCE CONTRIBUTIONS ACT.

**Fields, W. C.** 1879–1946. Actor and humorist. Born William Claude Dukenfield, Fields started as a juggler, then spent years on the musical stage before entering films. His curmudgeonly humor matched his raspy voice and bulbous nose.

*W. C. Fields*

**Fighting Irish** nickname of the University of Notre Dame FOOTBALL team.

**filling station** an automobile service station, providing motor fuel and other supplies and services for cars. An older term, but still widely used.

**Fillmore, Millard** 1800–1874. Thirteenth president of the United States (1850–1853).

**Finney, Charles Grandison** 1792–1875. Evangelist and theologian. Finney played an important role in the GREAT REVIVAL of the 19th century, which changed the religious and social landscape of the country. Finney's revivals emphasized emotional repentance and commitment to Jesus Christ.

**fireside chats** the homey radio addresses of FRANKLIN DELANO ROOSEVELT.

**first lady** informal title of the wife of a sitting U.S. president. The term originally also extended in the media to the children, relatives and even pets of the first family.

**First State** DELAWARE.

**First World** the industrialized world consisting of Japan, Australia, New Zealand, and the developed countries in North America and Europe.

**fish stick** a breaded and fried piece of fish that is shaped like a stick.

**Fitzgerald, F. Scott** 1896–1940. Novelist. The voice of the 1920s and the JAZZ AGE, Fitzgerald is best remembered for *The Great Gatsby* (1925), as well as lesser works such as his first novel, *This Side of Paradise* (1920), and the autobiographical *Tender Is the Night* (1934).

**Five Civilized Tribes** the five relatively Europeanized NATIVE AMERICAN tribes of the Southeastern United States: the Cherokee, Chickasaw, Choctaw, Creek, and Seminole. They were dispossessed of their lands by the United States government and forced to march to OKLAHOMA, where some of their descendants still live.

**Five Nations** the IROQUOIS LEAGUE of NATIVE AMERICAN tribes, consisting of the Cayuga, Mohawk, Oneida, Onondaga, and Seneca.

**five-and-dime** a type of department store, popular until the 1970s, featuring inexpensive goods. So called because many of its goods were originally priced at five or ten cents.

**Five-Foot-Shelf** the HARVARD CLASSICS.

**fizzbo** for sale by owner, property offered for sale without a broker or real estate agent.

**FL** FLORIDA. (The official two-letter post office abbreviation.)

**Flag Day** June 14, designated as Flag Day in 1949 in commemoration of the CONTINENTAL CONGRESS's adoption of the STARS AND STRIPES.

**flagship** the leader or the most important member in a group or the most profitable of a company's products.

**flame mail** hate E-MAIL sent or received on the INTERNET.

**Flamingo** a famous hotel/casino on THE STRIP in Las Vegas, NEVADA.

**flapjack** a PANCAKE.

**flapper** a young woman of the 1920s who dressed and behaved unconventionally. Flappers shocked society by smoking and drinking in public.

**flat tax** a nongraduated income tax at a fixed percentage of total income above a set minimum with no or few deductions. Advocated by some SUPPLY-SIDE economists.

**flat time sentence** a minimum prison sentence spelled out in law for certain

*flapper*

types of crimes, which cannot be reduced by the judge or through parole.

**flatliner** a flop or failure. From a flat line on an electrocardiogram indicating absence of life.

**flextime** a personnel practice in certain corporations that enables workers to choose their hours of work or stagger working hours according to need.

**Flickertail State** NORTH DAKOTA.

**flight capital** money that migrates from high-risk countries to low-risk countries.

**Florida** a state in the southeastern United States. Called the Sunshine State, its capital is Tallahassee and its largest city is Jacksonville. The mockingbird is Florida's state bird and the orange blossom is its state flower. Florida also includes the FLORIDA KEYS, a group of islands to the southwest of the state in the Gulf of Mexico. Abbreviated FL.

**Florida Keys** a group of islands southwest of FLORIDA. They include KEY WEST and Key Largo.

**flower children** members of the counterculture of the 1960s who used flowers and peace symbols as adornments. They were generally pacifists opposed to the VIETNAM WAR, and their slogan was "Make Love, Not War." Also called HIPPIES.

**Flying Wallendas** nickname of the Wallenda family, aerialists who performed with the Ringling Brothers and Barnum and Bailey Circus from 1928.

**FNMA** FEDERAL NATIONAL MORTGAGE ASSOCIATION.

**Foggy Bottom** the DEPARTMENT OF STATE.

**folk music** music of the common people that is handed down from generation to generation orally. American folk music developed from European forms brought to the colonies by early settlers.

**folk revival** a resurgence of FOLK MUSIC in the 1960s that combined ballads with protest music.

**folk rock** a blend of FOLK MUSIC and ROCK AND ROLL, generally folk lyrics set to a rock beat.

**follow spot** a bright spotlight used to track an actor's movements on the stage.

**Food and Drug Administration** a government agency within the DEPARTMENT OF HEALTH AND HUMAN SERVICES that monitors the purity and safety of food, cosmetics, and drugs; truth in packaging and labeling information; and sanitary practices in restaurants and other food-handling establishments. Abbreviated FDA.

**football** 1. a national sport developed in 1874 which has roots in rugby and soccer. It is played on a field by two teams of 11 members each, and consists of four quarters, each 15 minutes long. The game's objective is to score more goals, called TOUCHDOWNS, than the opposing team. Touchdowns are scored by getting the football past the opponent's goal line, either by running with it or passing it to another player who is across the line. Points can also be scored by kicking the ball past the goal posts. The first-place teams from each conference of the NATIONAL FOOTBALL LEAGUE play in the SUPER BOWL, the championship game. 2. the leather ball used to play the game of football. It is oval and pointed at each end.

**Ford, Gerald R.** 1913–. Thirty-eighth president of the United States (1974–1977).

**Ford, Henry** 1863–1947. Automobile manufacturer. A pioneer in his field, Ford organized the Ford Motor Company in 1903. His cost-cutting techniques and use of the assembly line enabled the company to produce inexpensive cars in mass quantities, soon making Ford the largest auto manufacturer in the world. More than fifteen million MODEL T Fords were sold before the model was discontinued in 1927. Ford's most notable failure was the EDSEL.

**Ford, John** 1895–1973. Film director. Ford won the ACADEMY AWARD five times, for *The Informer* (1935), *The Grapes of Wrath* (1940), *How Green Was My Valley* (1941), *The Quiet Man* (1952), and *The Last Hurrah* (1958).

**Ford's Theatre** theater in WASHINGTON, D.C. where JOHN WILKES BOOTH assassinated President ABRAHAM LINCOLN in 1865. Named after John T. Ford (1829–1894), its builder.

**forex** trading market for foreign currency. From foreign exchange.

**Formula One** racing car that has an engine of from 1,500 to 3,000 cubic centimeters displacement, with an open cockpit and open wheels.

**Fort Knox** 1. the legendary Treasury Department gold reserves depository located in an army post near Louisville, KENTUCKY. 2. any hoard of valuables.

**Fortune 500** the list of top U.S. corporations ranked on a variety of indicators, published annually by *Fortune* magazine, a magazine that analyzes business and industry.

**forty-niners** prospectors of gold who rushed to CALIFORNIA in 1849.

**Foster, Stephen** 1826–1864. Composer. Foster wrote some of the country's most beloved songs in the mid-19th century, such as "Oh! Susanna," "Jeanie with the Light Brown Hair," and "Old Folks at Home." Many of his songs were originally written for MINSTREL SHOWS.

**Founding Fathers** the collective name for the members of the CONSTITUTIONAL CONVENTION of 1787, particularly its more prominent members, such as GEORGE WASHINGTON, THOMAS JEFFERSON, ALEXANDER HAMILTON, and BENJAMIN FRANKLIN.

**4-H Clubs** youth organization founded in 1900 that promotes the four H's: head, heart, hands, and health. Started in ILLINOIS, it was taken over by the Department of Agriculture in 1914.

**400, The** media term for high society at the turn of the century. The term referred to the number of people who could fit into the ballroom of Mrs. William Astor, considered the arbiter of taste in her time.

**Fourteen Points** President WOODROW WILSON's plan for peace after WORLD WAR I. One of the points, "a general association of nations

**Fourth of July** the common term for INDEPENDENCE DAY, which falls on July 4. An official holiday, it is usually celebrated with fireworks.

**fractal** any of a class of irregular and odd shapes, surfaces, or curves produced by computer graphics programs.

**frame** an individual unit of a movie film. The standard movie speed is 24 frames per second.

**Franklin, Aretha** 1942–. Singer. Franklin, who recorded many SOUL MUSIC hits in the 1960s, is commonly called the *Queen of Soul*.

**Franklin, Benjamin** 1706–1790. American statesman and man of all talents. A printer, businessman, publisher, scientist, and politician, he was called the Wisest American of his time. He was one of the FOUNDING FATHERS.

**Franklin, John Hope** 1915–. Historian. The most prominent AFRICAN-AMERICAN historian and the first president of the Organization of American Historians.

**FRB** FEDERAL RESERVE BOARD.

*Benjamin Franklin*

**Freddie Mac** nickname for Federal Home Loan Mortgage Corporation.

**Free State** MARYLAND.

**Freedom Riders** African-American and white civil rights activists who challenged the laws on segregation in public transport in the early 1960s by riding together on buses.

**Freemason** a member of a fraternal organization, properly called Free and Accepted Masons, who follows certain secret rituals.

**Freesoilers** opponents of slavery in the 1840s who were later absorbed by the REPUBLICAN PARTY.

**freeway** an EXPRESSWAY on which no toll is collected. Compare with TOLLROAD.

**freeze frame** a still picture in a movie made by running a series of identical frames.

**French, Daniel Chester** 1850–1931. Sculptor. French produced some of the most famous public sculptures in America, including *The Minute Man* in Concord, MASSACHUSETTS, and the seated ABRAHAM LINCOLN in the LINCOLN MEMORIAL in WASHINGTON, D.C.

**(French) fries** fried strips of potato.

**Friedman, Milton** 1912–. Economist. Leader of the SUPPLY-SIDE or Chicago School of Economics, Friedman is the most articulate spokesman for the free market economy.

**Friends, Religious Society of** official name of the QUAKERS.

**Frisco** San Francisco, CALIFORNIA. (A nickname that is often resented by the residents of this city.)

**frontlash** a reaction to a backlash, especially a corrective against excesses generated by a backlash.

**Frost, Robert** 1874–1963. Poet. Frost won four PULITZER PRIZES for his work. A transplanted New Englander, his poems reflect the rugged beauty of the land.

**FSLIC** FEDERAL SAVINGS AND LOAN INSURANCE CORPORATION.

**FTC** FEDERAL TRADE COMMISSION.

**Fu Manchu mustache** a thin, drooping mustache that comes down vertically at the sides of the mouth. After Fu Manchu, a character in the mystery novels of author Sax Rohmer.

**fudge** a soft, rich candy made with butter, milk, sugar, and usually chocolate and nuts.

**Fulbright scholarship** a scholarship funded by the U.S. government for U.S. scholars to teach or do research abroad and for foreign scholars to do likewise in the United States. It was named after

Senator James William Fulbright of ARKANSAS, who sponsored the bill.

**full court press** a vigorous full-scale attack offensive in which all members of a team take part. Originally used in BASKETBALL.

**Fuller, Buckminster, Jr.** 1895–1983. Futurist. A brilliant, albeit eccentric, scientist, Fuller is best known for his invention of the geodesic dome, but his principal contributions to the 20th century are his extraordinary and original futurist ideas about Spaceship Earth.

**Fuller, Sarah Margaret** 1810–1850. Author, transcendentalist. One of the most brilliant female intellectuals of the 19th century, Fuller fought for equal rights for women, advocated TRANSCENDENTALISM, and was a major literary critic.

**Fulton, Robert** 1765–1815. Inventor. Fulton is best known for introducing the CLERMONT, the first commercially successful steamboat in America, in 1807.

**fundamentalist** a Christian committed to the literal inerrancy of the Bible and seeking to extend its authority in private and public life.

**funeral home** a business that prepares dead bodies for cremation or burial and usually plans and holds funeral services. Also called *funeral parlor*.

**funeral parlor** FUNERAL HOME.

**funk** popular music combining elements of JAZZ, BLUES, and SOUL MUSIC, marked by syncopated rhythm and a heavy, repetitive bass line.

**future shock** stress and disorientation caused by the rapid pace of technological and societal change. Coined by Alvin Toffler in his book *Future Shock*.

**futurology** the science of the future, especially the study of possible and probable futures and future trends. Also called futuristics.

# G

**G** See MOVIE RATINGS.

**GA** GEORGIA. (The official two-letter post office abbreviation.)

**Gable, Clark** 1901–1960. Actor. Good-looking and charming, Gable was one of the most popular movie actors of all time. His films include *It Happened One Night* (1934) and GONE WITH THE WIND (1939). Often called *The King*.

**Gadsden Purchase** a strip of land along the southern border of NEW MEXICO bought from Mexico in 1854 and named after railroad baron James Gadsden (1788–1858).

*Clark Gable*

**Gaia** a mythological name for planet Earth considered as a living organism that subsumes all living things.

**Galbraith, John Kenneth** 1908–. Economist. Galbraith is noted for his liberal version of American social and economic malaise. His *The Affluent Society* (1958) and *The New Industrial State* (1967) combined social satire with economic analysis and are among the most widely read books on economics.

**Gallaudet, Thomas Hopkins** 1787–1851. Educator. Gallaudet founded the first public school for the deaf, The American School for the Deaf, in Hartford, CONNECTICUT. His sons, Thomas and Edward, continued his work, establishing Gallaudet University, the first institution of higher education devoted entirely to the deaf.

**Gallup, George** 1901–1984. Pollster. Gallup was a pioneer in perfecting polling methods and forecasting the results of elections and making them a serious tool for social analysis.

**Gallup poll** a public opinion poll conducted by the Gallup organization, named after GEORGE GALLUP, who pioneered polling techniques.

**gangsta rap** a form of RAP MUSIC with lyrics extolling violence.

**GAO** GENERAL ACCOUNTING OFFICE.

**garage pop** informal pop music that combines elements of FOLK MUSIC and ROCK.

**garage sale** the sale of old and used household or personal belongings in or near the owner's garage.

**Garden State** NEW JERSEY.

**Garfield, James Abram** 1831–1881. Twentieth president of the United States (1881). Garfield was assassinated during his term in office.

**Garrison, William Lloyd** 1805–1879. Abolitionist. Garrison called for a complete and immediate end to slavery, and published the *Liberator*, an antislavery newspaper, from 1831 to 1865, until slavery was abolished.

**Garvey, Marcus** 1887–1940. AFRICAN-AMERICAN leader. Garvey sponsored the Back to Africa movement that stressed the separateness of black Americans. As founder of the Universal Negro Improvement Association in 1914, Garvey worked hard to make his fellow blacks self-reliant and economically independent.

**Gault** conferring legal protection and rights on minors. From the 1967 SUPREME COURT ruling in the case of Gerald Gault.

**Gay Nineties** the 1890s in American history, viewed as a period of peace and prosperity.

**gay rights** the civil rights of homosexuals, especially in the context of societal discrimination.

**GED** general equivalency diploma. A diploma awarded to someone who has met all the requirements for a high school diploma.

**Gem State** IDAHO.

**gender bender** a person or thing that tries to bridge gender differences by blending them.

**gender gap** disparity between the status of men and women in economy, society, education, and other sectors.

**General Accounting Office** the office of the legislative branch of the federal government that provides legal, accounting, and auditing services for the United States CONGRESS. Abbreviated GAO.

**Generation X** the post-BABY BOOM generation, whose members as a whole have values strikingly different from those of baby boomers. See also BABY BUST.

**gentleman farmer** a farm owner who does not do any farm work but instead hires others to do so.

**gentrification** the process of urban renewal by which inner cities are rebuilt to bring in more affluent residents.

**gentrify** to convert a working-class or poor neighborhood into a tony or expensive one in order to raise the property values.

**George, Henry** 1839–1897. Reformer. In his classic work, *Progress and Poverty* (1879), George proposed radical theories of income redistribution that remain valid even today.

**Georgia** a state in the southeastern United States. Known as the Peach State, its capital and largest city is Atlanta. Georgia's state bird is the brown thrasher and its state flower is the Cherokee rose. Abbreviated GA.

**gerrymander** to redraw electoral districts to increase a particular political party's chances at the polls. From Governor Elbridge Gerry (1744–1814) of MASSACHUSETTS, whose redrawn district resembled a salamander in shape.

**Gershwin, George** 1898–1937. Composer. Gershwin helped create 20th-century popular music, writing both concert pieces and musicals. His best-known works are the opera *Porgy and Bess* (1935) and *Rhapsody in Blue* (1924).

**Gettysburg Address** a brief speech by ABRAHAM LINCOLN at the dedication of a battlefield cemetery at Gettysburg, PENNSYLVANIA on November 19, 1863. It is the most famous speech in American history.

**ghost dance** a ritual dance practiced by Plains Indians in the 1880s to drive the white man from their lands. It led to the conflict at WOUNDED KNEE in which Chief SITTING BULL was killed.

**ghost town** one of many western towns established during the CALIFORNIA GOLD RUSH that were quickly deserted when no gold was found or the gold supply was depleted.

**GI** U.S. military personnel. From abbreviation of *Government Issue*, which is stamped on military uniforms and supplies.

**Gibson girl** a clean-cut, poised, athletic female ideal of the 1890s as created by illustrator Charles Dana Gibson (1867–1944).

**GIGO** Garbage In, Garbage Out, meaning what is put in is what comes out.

**Gilded Age** the period from the end of the CIVIL WAR to the turn of the century characterized by rapid economic growth and cultural renaissance.

**Gillespie, Dizzy** 1917–1993. Jazz musician. A trumpet virtuoso noted for his improvisations and technical skill, he, along with CHARLIE "BIRD" PARKER, led the BEBOP revolution.

**Gilman, Daniel Coit** 1831–1908. Educator. As president of the University of California (1872–1875) and the Johns Hopkins University (1875–1901), he was one of the shapers and movers of American higher education, emphasizing graduate training, research, and academic freedom.

**gimme cap** a rimmed cloth cap with the logo of a product or organization.

**Ginnie Mae** nickname of the GOVERNMENT NATIONAL MORTGAGE ASSOCIATION.

**Ginsberg, Allen** 1926–1997. Poet. A major poetic voice of the BEAT GENERATION who sought enlightenment in amplified sensory experience and anarchic individualism.

**git-fiddle** a folksy name for a guitar.

**glass ceiling** an intangible organizational barrier that blocks women and minorities from reaching top-level positions within a corporation.

**glitter rock** rock music whose performers wear glittering or decadent makeup and costumes.

**Global Positioning System** a technology for determining the position of an object anywhere in the world using a small hand-held receiver that picks up signals from a satellite network.

**global village** the world considered as a village or small place unified through electronic communications and a homogenized culture. Term coined by Canadian educator Marshall McLuhan (1911–1980).

**glossolalia** speaking in tongues, a biblically ordained practice followed by Pentecostal Christians.

**glyph** a process that creates a computer-readable bar code encoding certain types of information on paper in the form of diagonal marks in a stipple pattern.

**G-men** government men, specifically FBI agents, as well as members of the Bureau of Alcohol, Tobacco, and Firearms.

**GNMA** GOVERNMENT NATIONAL MORTGAGE ASSOCIATION.

**GNP** GROSS NATIONAL PRODUCT.

**Godfather** a MAFIA boss who heads a crime syndicate. Also known as *capo*.

**Godkin, Edwin Lawrence** 1831–1902. Reformer. One of the most influential journalists in the latter half of the 19th century, Godkin was founder and editor of *The Nation* and a spokesman for liberal reformers.

**go-go fund** an investment fund that engages in risky speculative stock market operations to maximize short-term profits.

**Goldberg, Rube** 1. 1883–1970. American cartoonist. His cartoons depicted various ingenious contraptions that were too complicated to work. 2. an elaborate and unworkable solution to a simple problem.

**Golden Arches** McDonald's, a fast-food restaurant chain. From the yellow *M* of the word *McDonald's*, usually a prominent feature on the restaurant's sign. (McDonald's is a trademarked name.)

**Golden Gate Bridge** a 4,200-foot bridge spanning the entrance to the San Francisco Bay, completed in 1937.

**Golden Gloves** the highest award in amateur boxing, presented by the Golden Gloves Association.

**golden parachute** a set of generous severance benefits paid to top executives who retire or are fired.

**Golden State** CALIFORNIA.

**Goldwyn, Samuel** 1882–1974. Film producer. Goldwyn was part of some of the best HOLLYWOOD studios, including MGM, Paramount, and United Artists. Among his many critically and commercially successful films was *The Best Years of Our Lives* (1946), which won seven ACADEMY AWARDS.

**Gompers, Samuel** 1850–1924. Labor leader. Founder and president of the American Federation of Labor for nearly 40 years from 1886, Gompers laid the foundation of the modern union movement in the United States.

***Gone with the Wind*** a best-selling novel by Margaret Mitchell (1900–1949) that won the PULITZER PRIZE in 1937 and became a famous motion picture in 1939. Set during the CIVIL WAR, the novel and film center around Scarlett O'Hara, a scheming SOUTHERN BELLE.

**gonzo journalism** journalism that is so inflammatory as to be a form of guerrilla warfare against conventional society. Coined by and associated with writer Hunter S. Thompson.

**Goodman, Benny** 1909–1986. Clarinetist and bandleader. Known as the King of Swing, Goodman ushered in the BIG BAND era with his lilting jazz tempos and seamless improvisation.

**Goodyear Blimp** a dirigible owned by the Goodyear Rubber Company and used for advertising purposes.

**GOP** Grand Old Party, nickname of the REPUBLICAN PARTY.

**gopher** a menu-based guide to directories on the INTERNET, arranged by subject.

*Goodyear Blimp*

**Gopher State** MINNESOTA.

**gospel music** energetic religious music that evolved from Negro spirituals, the BLUES, and white hymns.

**Gotham** New York City.

**Government National Mortgage Association** the government agency that purchases mortgages and sells interest in securities backed by these mortgages to the public. Usually referred to as Ginnie Mae. Abbreviated GNMA.

**GPA** GRADE POINT AVERAGE.

**Graceland** ELVIS PRESLEY'S mansion in Memphis, TENNESSEE.

**grade point average** a numerical conversion of letter grades used to rank students. A grade of A is usually either 4.0 or 5.0, depending on the scale. A GPA figure is often followed by the value of an A. Often found on résumés and college entrance applications.

**Graham, Billy** 1918–. Evangelist. Graham's crusades around the world, along with his preaching on both television and radio, led to thousands of commitments to Christ.

**Graham, Martha** 1894–1991. Choreographer, dancer. Describing her dance as an affirmation of life, Graham turned modern dance into an art form on a par with ballet and lifted it from the vaudeville stage to the concert hall.

**Grammy** a gold-plated replica of an old-fashioned phonograph, presented as an award to the year's outstanding musical albums and recording artists by the National Academy of Recording Arts and Sciences.

**Grammy Awards** the annual awards presented since 1958 to the best in the music industry by the National Academy of Recording Arts and Sciences. From gramaphone, record player.

**Grand Canyon** a spectacular river gorge in northern ARIZONA measuring about 18 miles across, 200 miles long, and more than one mile from its rim to the Colorado River at the bottom.

**Grand Canyon State** ARIZONA.

**Grand Ole Opry** a television, radio, and stage show showcasing COUNTRY MUSIC in Nashville, TENNESSEE. It is the home of COUNTRY MUSIC in the United States.

**Grand Tetons** a mountain range in northwest WYOMING, part of the ROCKY MOUNTAINS.

**Grange, National** an organization of rural interests founded in 1867. Its full name is the National Grange of Patrons of Husbandry.

**Granite State** NEW HAMPSHIRE.

**granny dumping** the abandonment of elderly and infirm persons by their children or grandchildren.

**granny glasses** gold or steel-rimmed eyeglasses, as worn by elderly matrons.

**granola** a mixture of dry oats, brown sugar, nuts, and raisins, eaten as a health food.

**Grant, Ulysses S.** 1822–1885. Eighteenth president of the United States (1869–1877). Grant, a UNION general in the CIVIL WAR, was called the AMERICAN SPHINX.

**Grant's Tomb** the tomb that holds the remains of ULYSSES S. GRANT and his wife, located in New York City.

**GRAS** Generally Recognized As Safe, a label used by the FOOD AND DRUG ADMINISTRATION to indicate food ingredients not harmful to humans.

*Ulysses S. Grant*

**Grauman's Chinese Theater** the original name of a HOLLYWOOD movie theater famous for the footprints or handprints of movie stars in cement near the entrance.

**Great Awakening** an evangelistic revival in the early 18th century led by JONATHAN EDWARDS in MASSACHUSETTS. Among its lasting legacies are PRINCETON UNIVERSITY and Rutgers University.

**Great Books** a reading program established at the University of Chicago by educators Robert Maynard Hutchins (1899–1977) and Mortimer Adler (1902– ), including many of the great literary classics of the Western World.

**Great Depression** the worst economic depression in the history of the United States, it began on BLACK TUESDAY in 1929 and continued until the 1940s. Millions of Americans were unemployed during this period.

**Great Lakes** the five glacial lakes that separate the United States from Canada: Ontario, Erie, Huron, Michigan, and Superior. Together, they are the largest body of freshwater in the world.

**Great Plains** the flat grasslands running from TEXAS to Canada and from the Mississippi Valley to the ROCKY MOUNTAINS. It was the home of the Plains Indians and the buffalo hunters.

**Great Revival** an evangelistic revival of the early 19th century led by Presbyterian minister and evangelist James McGready (1758–1817), who pioneeered the CAMP MEETING. Also known as the *Kentucky Revival* or the *Second Awakening*.

**Great Society** President LYNDON BAINES JOHNSON's domestic agenda containing a series of social reforms directed at eliminating poverty and race discrimination.

**Great Triumvirate** the three most famous orators in the U.S. Senate: John C. Calhoun (1782–1850), Henry Clay (1777–1852), and Daniel Webster (1782–1852).

**Great White Way** BROADWAY in New York City because of the dazzling bright lights at night.

**Greatest Show on Earth** the promotional slogan of the BARNUM AND BAILEY circus.

**Green Berets** the Special Forces, an elite unit of the U.S. Army. Named for its headgear, it played a notable role in the VIETNAM WAR.

**green card** a card that identifies resident aliens in the United States.

**Green Mountain State** VERMONT.

**green room** a backstage room in a theater where actors await their cue or call.

**green thumb** an innate skill at getting plants to grow, considered as a physical trait. The opposite of BROWN THUMB.

**Greenpeace** an environmental organization actively opposing measures that are likely to damage animal life on land and in the sea.

**Greenwich Village** a New York City neighborhood where New York University and Washington Square Park are located. It is considered New York's equivalent of the Left Bank in Paris because of its large number of creative residents who lead bohemian lifestyles.

**Grey, Zane** 1875–1939. Prolific novelist of the American West.

**griddle cake** PANCAKE.

**gridiron** FOOTBALL field.

**gridlock** the paralysis of traffic at intersections of major urban thoroughfares because vehicles are unable to move.

**Griffith, D. W.** 1875–1948. Film producer. Griffith's three-hour film, *Birth of a Nation* (1915), is considered one of the greatest silent films of all time.

**grinder** SUB(MARINE SANDWICH).

**gringo** a disparaging Mexican term for white North Americans. From Spanish *griego*, stranger.

**grip** a stagehand who helps move scenery or works at other odd jobs.

**grits** coarsely ground cornmeal, boiled and eaten as a breakfast cereal. (This is found throughout the southeastern United States and not widely known elsewhere.)

**gross national product** a measure of economic welfare determined by the total value of a country's output of goods and services. Abbreviated GNP.

**ground zero** the area where a catastrophic event takes place and from where the shock waves radiate.

**Groundhog Day** February 2, when, according to folklore, groundhogs emerge from their dens and determine the length of the remaining winter. If a groundhog sees its shadow, it returns underground for another six weeks of winter; if it sees no shadow, it betokens an early spring.

**grubstake** 1. money for supplies, loaned to a prospector with the expectation that the lender will receive part of the value of whatever is discovered. (Especially during the last century in the southwestern United States. Often provided as a speculative loan.) 2. to provide someone with needed supplies on loan.

**grunge** 1. a loud, sometimes chaotic, form of rock music that features distorted guitars. 2. a fashion trend among young people in the late 1980s and 1990s, characterized by old (or old-looking) and often oversized clothes, such as worn flannel shirts, big shorts, and torn jeans.

**GU** GUAM. (The official two-letter post office abbreviation.)

**Guam** a U.S. territory, it is the largest of the Mariana Islands. Its capital and largest city is Agana. Abbreviated GU.

**Gulf War** PERSIAN GULF WAR.

**Gullah** 1. a group of AFRICAN-AMERICANS inhabiting the Sea Islands and coastal districts of SOUTH CAROLINA and GEORGIA who have successfully preserved some of their ancestral African speech forms and culture. 2. the language spoken by the Gullah.

**gumbo** a spicy seafood or meat soup of African origin deriving its flavor from okra.

**Gun that Won the West** nickname applied to the Colt .44 revolver and the Winchester 73 repeating rifle, both used by pioneers in the American West.

**Guthrie, Woody** 1912–1967. Folksinger and songwriter. Known affectionately as Woody, Guthrie was one of the greatest singers of the FOLK REVIVAL and is best remembered for such songs as "This Land is Your Land" and "Reuben James."

# H

**hacker** a computer whiz or buff, especially one who is proficient in manipulating computer programs.

**Haggard, Merle** 1937–. Country singer and songwriter. Haggard gained fame for his anticounterculture song "Okie from Muskogee."

**Haight-Ashbury** a residential section of San Francisco, CALIFORNIA, that gained notoriety in the 1960s as a haven for FLOWER CHILDREN and the drug counterculture.

**"Hail, Columbia"** a patriotic song written in 1798 by Joseph Hopkinson and set to music by Philip Phile.

**"Hail to the Chief"** a march written in 1812 by Sir Walter Scott, used to announce the arrival of the U.S. president.

**ham radio** amateur radio, a hobby in which people contact each other by radio.

**hamburger** 1. ground beef. (This has nothing to do with ham but is from the German city of Hamburg, where pounded beef steak was once a favorite food.) 2. a patty made of ground beef. 3. a sandwich made of a hamburger patty on a specially shaped bun. The most popular American sandwich, the hamburger is usually accompanied by the condiments mustard, ketchup, sliced onion, pickles, and sometimes tomato and lettuce. When a slice of cheese is added, the result is a cheeseburger. 4. a stupid-acting person with no more sense than a pile of ground meat. (Slang. Also an insulting term of address.)

**hamburger stand**  1. a vendor's wagon or counter where HAMBURGERS are sold. (Typically at a sports stadium or game, a fair, or other outdoor event.) 2. any small diner or café that specializes in hamburgers and similar food. 3. any cheap place of business.

**Hamilton, Alexander**
1757–1804. American statesman. One of the FOUNDING FATHERS and a member of the CONTINENTAL CONGRESS, Hamilton advocated a strong central government. He contributed to THE FEDERALIST and urged the ratification of the CONSTITUTION. He was killed in 1804 in a duel with AARON BURR, then vice president of the United States.

*Alexander Hamilton*

**Hammerstein, Oscar II**
1895–1960. Lyricist. Hammerstein, BROADWAY's most distinguished lyricist, along with his colleague RICHARD RODGERS, produced several classics of the musical theater, including *Oklahoma!* (1943), *South Pacific* (1949), *The King and I* (1951), and *The Sound of Music* (1959).

**Hammett, Dashiell**  1894–1961. Author. A leader of the HARD-BOILED FICTION school, Hammett created a number of suspenseful detective classics, including 1930's *The Maltese Falcon* (with Sam Spade as the detective) and 1932's *The Thin Man*.

**hammock**  a programming slot between two popular shows, used to launch a new program.

**Hancock, John**  1737–1793. Statesman. Hancock was the president of the CONTINENTAL CONGRESS and the first to sign the DECLARATION OF INDEPENDENCE. His large and conspicuous signature on the document led to the use of *John Hancock* as a colloquial term for one's signature.

**Hanna and Barbera** cartoonists William Hanna (1910–) and Joseph Barbera (1911–), producers of *The Flintstones* and other animated cartoons for MGM.

**"Happy Days are Here Again"** Democratic campaign song and the NEW DEAL theme song, composed in 1929 by Milton Ager and Jack Yellen.

**happy hour** a time set apart in bars and cocktail lounges during early evenings when alcoholic drinks are served at reduced prices.

**Happy Warrior** nickname of Alfred E. Smith (1873–1944), governor of NEW YORK and losing Democratic presidential candidate in 1928.

**hard copy** the printout of a text generated in a computer or word processor.

**hard science** any of the natural or physical sciences, such as physics or chemistry. Distinguished from SOFT SCIENCE.

**hard-boiled fiction** detective fiction of the 1920s and 1930s marked by brute realism and terse writing. Two of its great practitioners were RAYMOND CHANDLER and DASHIELL HAMMETT.

**Harding, Warren G.** 1865–1923. Twenty-ninth president of the United States (1921–1923). Harding died in office in 1923.

**Harlem** the urban ghetto of New York City, originally a Dutch farm community called Nieuw Haarlem.

**Harlem Renaissance** the literary era associated with notable Harlem writers, such as LANGSTON HUGHES and Zora Neale Hurston (1901–1960).

*Harper's* a literary magazine, founded in New York in the mid-19th century as *Harper's New Monthly Magazine*, by Harper Brothers, publishers.

**Harris, Joel Chandler** 1848–1908. Journalist and short story writer. Best known for his Uncle Remus stories, Chandler created a new genre of fiction based on AFRICAN-AMERICAN folklore.

**Harrison, Benjamin** 1833–1901. Twenty-third president of the United States (1889–1893).

**Harrison, William Henry** 1773–1841. Ninth president of the United States (1841).

**Harvard Classics** a set of great books, assembled by CHARLES WILLIAM ELIOT, president of HARVARD UNIVERSITY. Also called the *Five-Foot-Shelf.*

**Harvard University** the first university in the British colonies in North America, located in Cambridge, MASSACHUSETTS. Founded in 1636, and named after John Harvard, its British benefactor, it is now the richest university in the IVY LEAGUE.

**hash browns** chopped or shredded potatoes fried crisp.

**hash mark** any of the broken markers or lines on a FOOTBALL field.

**Hassam, Frederick Childe** 1859–1935. Painter. A leading American impressionist, Hassam painted busy street scenes and sunlit gardens in the manner of Claude Monet.

**Hatfields and McCoys** two APPALACHIAN MOUNTAIN clans noted for their long-standing, violent feud which began during the CIVIL WAR when the KENTUCKY McCoys fought on the UNION side and the WEST VIRGINIA Hatfields on the CONFEDERATE side. Between 85 and 200 lives were lost before the feud ebbed in the 1880s.

**Hawaii** a U.S. state located in the Pacific Ocean, composed of islands. Called the Aloha State, its capital and largest city is Honolulu. Hawaii's state flower is the hibiscus and its state bird is the nene. It was the last state to be admitted to the United States (1959). Abbreviated HI.

**Hawaiian-Aleutian standard time** the standard time in the Hawaiian and Aleutian Islands. It is ten hours behind Greenwich time and two hours behind PACIFIC STANDARD TIME. Abbreviated HST.

**hawk** a person who favors a strong U.S. military posture or involvement in military actions abroad.

**Hawkeye State** IOWA.

**Hawthorne, Nathaniel** 1804–1864. Novelist. Hawthorne dug deep into the legends and lore of Puritan NEW ENGLAND to produce many classic tales, including *The Scarlet Letter* (1850) and *The House of the Seven Gables* (1851).

**Hawthorne Effect** the improvement in the morale, productivity or efficiency of workers when they realize that their performance is being watched or evaluated. From Hawthorne Works of the Western Electric Company in ILLINOIS, where an experiment to boost productivity and quality was held in the 1920s.

**Hayes, Helen** 1900–1993. Actress. Hayes dominated the New York stage for more than 60 years, beginning at the age of five and making her last stage appearance in 1971.

**Hayes, Rutherford B.** 1822–1893. Nineteenth president of the United States (1877–1881).

**Hays Code** See HAYS OFFICE.

**Hays Office** the informal name for the Motion Picture Producers and Distributors of America, founded in 1922 as a watchdog organization to monitor and enforce ethical standards in the industry. It was initially headed by Will Hays (1879–1954), whose office drafted a production code that stayed in effect from 1934 to 1966. The Hays Code banned profanity, drug trafficking, and nudity in movies.

**Haywood, William ("Big Bill")** See INDUSTRIAL WORKERS OF THE WORLD.

**HBO** Home Box Office, a major cable television network available to subscribers. HBO broadcasts both new and old movies via satellite, and also produces its own movies, documentaries, and specials.

**HDTV** high-definition television. A television standard that offers greater clarity and resolution by increasing the number of scan lines.

**headhunter** an executive recruiter.

**heads up display** a visual display of instrument readings on an automobile windshield enabling a driver to read data without taking his or her eyes off the road. Also found in aircraft.

**health maintenance organization** a prepaid health care plan that employs a diverse medical staff to offer a comprehensive array of health services. Abbreviated HMO.

**health spa** a commercial gymnasium containing exercise machines designed to help in weight reduction and body fitness.

**Hearst, William Randolph** 1863–1951. Newspaper magnate who, at the height of his career in the 1920s, headed an empire of 20 newspapers from his CALIFORNIA estate, SAN SIMEON.

**heavy metal** a loud form of rock music featuring flashy guitar work, unnaturally high-pitched male vocals, and morbid lyrics.

**hedonic damages** damages claimed in a civil suit for the loss of the ability to enjoy life's pleasures.

**Heinlein, Robert Anson** 1907–1988. Author. The dean of science fiction writers, Heinlein transformed the genre from an escapist device into a serious effort to describe the future.

**Heisman Trophy** annual award for the best FOOTBALL player chosen by a panel of sportscasters. Established in 1935 by the New York City Downtown Athletic Club and named in honor of its president, John W. Heisman (1869–1936).

**helipad** a landing and takeoff area for helicopters.

**Hellman, Lillian** 1905–1984. Playwright. Hellman's controversial but successful plays included *The Little Foxes* (1939). Along with her lover, DASHIELL HAMMETT, she defied the HOUSE UN-AMERICAN ACTIVITIES COMMITTEE during the MCCARTHY ERA.

**Hell's Angels** a CALIFORNIA-based motorcyle gang of outlaws whose logo is a winged skull.

**Hemingway, Ernest** 1899–1961. Novelist. Affectionately known as "Papa," Hemingway is the quintessential American writer and the most representative of the LOST GENERATION of American writers. His works include *The Sun Also Rises* (1926), *A Farewell to Arms* (1929), *For Whom The Bell Tolls* (1940), and *The Old Man and the Sea* (1952). A rugged individualist who glorified macho qualities as a fighter and lover, his works defined an entire generation. He won the PULITZER PRIZE in 1953 and the Nobel Prize for Literature in 1954.

**Hendrix, Jimi** 1942–1970. Guitarist and songwriter. Hendrix expanded the horizons of rock music through his inimitable virtuosity in improvising sounds with his electric guitar. His music was violent and troubled yet at the same time sensual and triumphant.

*Jimi Hendrix (center)*

**Henri, Robert** See ASHCAN SCHOOL.

**Henry, Joseph** 1797–1878. Scientist. Known for his work on electricity, he made notable contributions to electromagnetism and invented types of galvanometers. As the first secretary and director of the SMITHSONIAN INSTITUTION, he stressed scientific research.

**Hepburn, Katharine** 1909–. Hepburn, known for her spunky personality both onscreen and off, won four ACADEMY AWARDS for Best Actress. Her career spanned decades and included roles in *The Philadelphia Story* (1940), *The African Queen* (1951), and *On Golden Pond* (1981).

**Hermitage** ANDREW JACKSON's plantation home near Nashville, TENNESSEE.

**hero (sandwich)** a SUB(MARINE SANDWICH).

**hex signs** circular symbols appearing on PENNSYLVANIA DUTCH barns, believed to have the power of warding off evil.

**HHS** DEPARTMENT OF HEALTH AND HUMAN SERVICES.

**HI** HAWAII. (The official two-letter post office abbreviation.)

**Hiawatha** an Indian prophet who helped to found the IROQUOIS LEAGUE. His legend was the inspiration for the poem *Song of Hiawatha* by HENRY WADSWORTH LONGFELLOW.

**high five** an informal gesture in which two people greet or congratulate each other by slapping their raised palms together.

**highball** an alcoholic drink, usually made with whiskey and soda.

**Hill** CONGRESS; the legislative branch of the U.S. government. From CAPITOL HILL, where CONGRESS meets.

**hillbilly** a person from the backwoods or mountains, typically from the Southeastern United States or the Ozark Mountains. (This is usually used in an insulting fashion. The *hill* part refers to mountains and the *billy* is probably from the name *Billy*, used as a generic for *fellow*, as with *Bud* or *Mac*.)

**hip-hop** the cultural context of RAP MUSIC, dominated by the clothing and the speech patterns of the streets.

**hippie** a member of the 1960s counterculture who cultivated an alternative and self-indulgent lifestyle opposing participation in mainstream society and the VIETNAM WAR and favoring Eastern religions, use of marijuana, and free sex. Also spelled *hippy*.

***His Master's Voice*** an 1898 painting by Francis Barraud showing his dog peering curiously into the horn of an old-style record player. In 1901 the image and the legend were adopted as trademark of the Victor Talking Machine Company, which was later taken over by RCA in 1929.

**Hispanic** a Spanish speaker of Latin American descent or ancestry living in the United States.

**hit** a unit that measures website use, expressed as a one-time access by one user.

**Hitchcock, Alfred** 1899–1980. Director. Known as the Master of Suspense, Hitchcock was one of the preeminent directors in HOLLYWOOD, known for his mastery of the cinematic technique. Among his classics were *Suspicion* (1941), *Spellbound* (1945), *Dial M for Murder* (1954), *Rear Window* (1954), *North by Northwest* (1959), and *Psycho* (1960).

*Alfred Hitchcock*

**HMO** HEALTH MAINTENANCE ORGANIZATION.

**hoagie** a SUB(MARINE SANDWICH).

**hobo** an itinerant and impecunious laborer.

**hog jowl** the cheek of the pig, eaten as food. Considered a southern poor people's food with little appeal in the rest of the country.

**holding pattern** the circular pattern of flight of an airplane awaiting clearance for landing from the air traffic control tower.

**Holiday, Billie** 1915–1959. Singer. An original JAZZ singer with a smoky and emotional voice, Holiday, often called Lady Day, became the model for succeeding jazz singers.

**Hollywood** 1. a district located in the city of Los Angeles, CALIFORNIA, known as the center of the motion-picture industry for many years. It was first used as a film location in 1913. Also known as *Tinseltown*. 2. having the characteristics of the glamour, glitter, and pretensions of Hollywood, CALIFORNIA. 3. someone—usually a male—who is suave and pretentious in the manner of a Hollywood star.

**Holmes, Oliver Wendell** 1809–1894. Essayist, physician, and poet. Holmes exemplified the best New England intellectual traditions and adorned 19th-century literature with his wit, common sense, and learning. He is best known for *The Autocrat at the Breakfast Table* (1858).

**Holocaust** the destruction of European Jewry by Nazis during WORLD WAR II.

**home run** in BASEBALL, when a batter hits a pitched ball out of the stadium or past a certain distance within the stadium, so that all runners on base can score.

**home school** a system under which parents who do not wish to send their children to public or private schools teach them at home according to a prescribed curriculum approved by the state.

**Homer, Winslow** 1836–1910. Painter. Homer was a naturalist painter who specialized in CIVIL WAR scenes and seascapes.

**Homestead Act**  an 1862 law that granted 160 acres of western land free to any potential HOMESTEADER who agreed to live on it for at least five years.

**homesteader**  a person who settled on a tract of land under the HOMESTEAD ACT.

**hominy (grits)**  1. hulled kernels of dried corn, to be boiled and eaten as food. 2. boiled kernels of dried corn, eaten as a breakfast dish. (See also GRITS.)

**homophobia**  fear of homosexuals and of being tainted by their association.

**honcho**  the boss or chief of a group.

**honky-tonk**  a seedy saloon and dance hall that purveys both drinks and entertainment.

**hoosier**  a native of INDIANA; a resident of INDIANA. (Speculation as to the origin of this word has provided much entertainment over the years. The origin is unknown, but it may be related to an English dialect word meaning "large.")

**Hoosier State**  INDIANA.

**hootenanny**  an informal FOLK MUSIC gathering in which the audience participates in the singing.

**Hoover Dam**  a dam in the COLORADO RIVER located near the town of Boulder at the border between NEVADA and ARIZONA. Dedicated in 1935, the dam provides electric power and helps control flooding. LAKE MEAD was created by the dam. Once also called Boulder Dam by people who were opposed to HERBERT HOOVER, the former American president for whom the dam is named.

**Hoover, Herbert**  1874–1964. Thirty-first president of the United States (1929–1933). Hoover was president during the early part of the GREAT DEPRESSION.

**Hooverville**  a shack city for the urban homeless, built during the administration of President HERBERT HOOVER.

**Hopi**  an Indian people of northeastern ARIZONA, noted for their Kachina dolls and snake dances.

**Hopper, Edward** 1882–1967. Painter. Hopper was a figurative painter distinguished for solitary figures in sparse interiors or urban settings.

**hornbook** a form of primer used in Colonial America consisting of a leaf of paper containing the alphabet, the 10 digits and the Lord's Prayer protected by a translucent plate of horn and mounted on a tablet of wood with a handle.

**hot dog** 1. a frankfurter sausage, eaten alone, in a sandwich, or with other foods such as baked beans. 2. a sandwich consisting of a frankfurter or wiener on a special long bun, with additional condiments such as mustard, onions, pickles, chili, peppers, and ketchup. (This sandwich is easy to hold in one's hand, making it popular at sporting events.) 3. (Usually hot dog or hot-dog) to show off; to exhibit one's athletic skills. 4. (Usually Hot dog!) Wow! (An exclamation.)

**hotcake** a PANCAKE.

**hothouse** to start home schooling of children at an early age in order to give them a head start when they join a kindergarten.

**Houdini, Harry** 1874–1926. Magician. Born Erich Weiss, he is considered the greatest escape artist in history.

**House of Representatives** the lower house of CONGRESS. Each state is allowed a certain number of REPRESENTATIVES, based on its population. The Speaker of the House, who is elected by its members, presides over the House.

**House Un-American Activities Committee** a House investigative committee formed in 1938 to ferret out Nazis and later, after the end of WORLD WAR II, Communists. Abbreviated HUAC.

**Housing and Urban Development** an executive department of the United States government in charge of administering mortgage programs to enable people to own homes, aiding in construction and renovation of housing, aiding low-income families who cannot afford rent, and working to abolish discrimination in housing. Abbreviated HUD.

**Houston, Samuel** 1793–1863. President of the Republic of Texas (1836–1838 and 1841–1844) and later governor of the state of TEXAS. The city of Houston, TEXAS, was named after him.

**Howe, Julia Ward** 1819–1910. Reformer. Howe was a leader in the woman's suffrage movement, and is best known as the composer of "THE BATTLE HYMN OF THE REPUBLIC."

**Howells, William Dean** 1837–1920. Critic, novelist, editor. As editor of the *Atlantic Monthly* from 1871 to 1881, Howells was one of the most influential literary figures of his era. His own output included 35 novels (including *The Rise of Silas Lapham*, 1885), 8 story anthologies, 35 plays, 5 books of poetry, 6 books of criticism, and 34 miscellaneous volumes.

**HST** HAWAIIAN-ALEUTIAN STANDARD TIME.

**HUAC** HOUSE UN-AMERICAN ACTIVITIES COMMITTEE.

**HUD** HOUSING AND URBAN DEVELOPMENT.

**Hudson River** an important waterway that rises in northeast NEW YORK and flows south to New York City. Named for English explorer Henry Hudson.

**Hudson River school** a group of painters whose evocative paintings of the American landscape, particularly of the Hudson Valley, made them the masters of this genre. Among the more prominent members of this school were THOMAS COLE, ASHER B. DURAND, and Frederick Edwin Church (1826–1900).

**Hughes, Langston** 1902–1967. Poet, novelist, and playwright. A versatile writer, Hughes captured the essence of the black experience in the pre-Civil Rights era and was a key figure in the HARLEM RENAISSANCE.

**hula** a Hawaiian pantomime story dance.

**hush puppy** a small, oblong cake of cornmeal—sometimes with onions—fried in deep fat. (The name is sometimes said to be from the practice of

*hula dancers*

tossing this cake to the family dogs to keep them quiet while supper was being cooked.)

**husking bee**  a social gathering for the communal husking of corn. Before there were machines to do this job, members of the community gathered to remove the husks from corncobs by hand.

**hustle**  a lively dance for couples set to DISCO music, marked by intricate footwork, dips, and spins.

**Hutchins, Robert Maynard**  1899–1977. Educator. Named president of the University of Chicago at the age of 30, Hutchins made humanities an essential part of the university curriculum and instituted the GREAT BOOKS program with Mortimer J. Adler (1902–). Later he headed the Center for the Study of Democratic Institutions.

**Hutchinson, Anne Marbury**  1591–1643. Religious leader. She was convicted of heresy by the PURITANS and banished to RHODE ISLAND.

**Hyde Park**  small town on the banks of the Hudson near Poughkeepsie, NEW YORK, where the FDR home and the CORNELIUS VANDERBILT mansion are located.

**hypertext**  highlighted words that link INTERNET documents to related documents.

# I

**IA** IOWA. (The official two-letter post office abbreviation.)

**IBM** International Business Machine Corporation, a leading computer manufacturer. It is nicknamed *Big Blue*.

**ICC** INTERSTATE COMMERCE COMMISSION.

**icebox** a refrigerator. From the time when home refrigeration was accomplished with ice delivered to the home.

**icon** a graphic image on a computer screen representing a function or an option available to the user when clicked on with a mouse.

**ID** IDAHO. (The official two-letter post office abbreviation.)

**Idaho** a state of the western United States, located in the ROCKY MOUNTAINS. Known as the Panhandle State, the Gem State, or the Spud State (for its potato production), Idaho's capital and largest city is Boise. The mountain bluebird is its state bird and the syringa is the state flower. Abbreviated ID.

**identity crisis** a developmental personality disturbance especially during adolescence when a person is confused by changes taking place in body and mind, becomes anxious about the kind of person he or she wants to be, and is unable to achieve inner and outer coherence.

**Iditarod** an 1,100-mile dogsled race, the longest in the world, held every March in ALASKA.

**Ike** DWIGHT DAVID EISENHOWER.

**IL** ILLINOIS. (The official two-letter post office abbreviation.)

**Illinois** a state in the U.S. MIDWEST. Called the Prairie State or the Land of Lincoln, its capital is Springfield and its largest city is Chicago. The cardinal is the state bird of Illinois and the violet is its state flower. Abbreviated IL.

**immersion method** an intensive course of oral instruction, especially in a foreign language, in which students are forced to give up communicating in any other language.

**imperial presidency** a strong presidency, such as that of FRANKLIN DELANO ROOSEVELT, under which the office becomes invested with autocratic powers not sanctioned by the CONSTITUTION.

**impresario** the producer or director of a play or other type of entertainment.

**IN** INDIANA. (The official two-letter post office abbreviation.)

**In God We Trust** national motto of the United States since 1956.

**in the loop** actively participating in or having access to a chain of authority or responsibility.

**in your face** insensitive, aggressive, and confrontational.

**Independence Day** July 4, a national holiday celebrating the country's independence from England. Commonly called FOURTH OF JULY.

**Independence Hall** a Georgian-style building in Philadelphia whose central tower once housed the LIBERTY BELL and where the CONTINENTAL CONGRESS met in 1776 and adopted the DECLARATION OF INDEPENDENCE.

**index crime** any of the seven serious crimes on which detailed statistics are published by the FBI in its Uniform Crime Reports. Of the seven, four are crimes of personal violence (murder, aggravated assault, rape, and robbery), and the other three are property crimes (burglary, larceny of $50 or more, and auto theft).

**Indian** one of the indigenous people of the Americas, or one of their descendants. *Native American* is now the preferred term.

**Indiana** a state in the U.S. MIDWEST. Known as the Hoosier State, its capital and largest city is Indianapolis. Its state bird is the cardinal and state flower is the peony. Abbreviated IN.

**Indianapolis 500** the 500-mile automobile race for FORMULA ONE cars held each MEMORIAL DAY in Indianapolis, INDIANA, since 1911.

**individual retirement account** a retirement plan that allows a certain portion of one's annual income to be placed in a special account. No taxes are due on the earnings until retirement. Abbreviated IRA.

**Industrial Workers of the World** a radical labor confederation founded in 1905 in Chicago, ILLINOIS, by a convention of delegates, including labor leaders WILLIAM ("BIG BILL") HAYWOOD and EUGENE DEBS.

**infomercial** a commercial that emphasizes consumer-oriented information rather than product promotion.

**infotainment** a television program that combines entertainment and information elements.

**Inge, William Motter** 1913–1973. Novelist, playwright. Inge, a PULITZER PRIZE-winning playwright, set many of his plays in the MIDWEST, projecting Midwestern values and lifestyles.

**ink-jet printer** a high-speed printer in which jets of ink are broken into magnetized droplets and deflected by an internal computer to form letters and numbers on paper.

**inner city** the core section in older cities characterized by poverty and overcrowding.

**inning** in BASEBALL, a period of playing time that is terminated after the two teams have received three outs each while up to bat. The two halves of an inning are called the top and the bottom.

**insider trading** the illegal practice of buying and selling of stocks by corporate officials or their friends and colleagues on the basis of privileged or confidential information not available to the public.

**instant book** a book dealing with a sensational event or a celebrity produced quickly by cutting short the lead time.

**intelligent document** a paper document that contains printed text as well as coded compuuter-readable information.

**intentional community** a self-sustaining private community with its own police force and other social services.

**interactive** allowing the viewer to actively participate in a computer program on the screen or change its outcome.

**Internal Revenue Service** the federal agency responsible for collecting federal taxes. It is part of the Department of the Treasury. Abbreviated IRS.

**Internet** a digital system of high-speed global communication and data transfer, which developed from a military project in the 1960s.

**Interstate Commerce Commission** a government agency that regulates commerce across state lines. Abbreviated ICC.

**interstate highway** a highway that runs through different states, connecting major American cities.

**intrapreneur** a corporate executive who is authorized to act as an entrepreneur and undertake new ventures which, if profitable, will revert to the parent company.

**Iowa** a state in the U.S. MIDWEST. Iowa's capital and largest city is Des Moines. Iowa is known as the Hawkeye State. Its state bird is the eastern goldfinch and its state flower is the wild rose. Abbreviated IA.

**IRA** INDIVIDUAL RETIREMENT ACCOUNT.

**iron horse** a Plains Indian term for a railroad.

**Iroquois League** a political confederacy of important Indian tribes, originally five and later six, formed in the 16th century under the leadership of Deganawidah and HIAWATHA. The original five members were the Cayuga, Oneida, Onondaga, Mohawk, and Seneca, and the sixth member was the Tuscarora.

**IRS** INTERNAL REVENUE SERVICE.

**Irving, Washington** 1783–1859. Author. The first important author in American literary history, Irving was a prolific writer whose output includes the classic tales "Rip Van Winkle" and "The Legend of Sleepy Hollow."

**ISBN**  International Standard Book Number, an identifying number printed on all books.

**ISDN**  Integrated Services Digital Network, a telecommunications network that speeds communications by digitizing content.

**ISO-9000**  a set of acceptable global quality standards that ensures the continuous elimination of product defects.

**ISSN**  International Standard Serial Number, an identifying number printed on all journals and serials.

**It Girl**  nickname of CLARA BOW.

**ITA**  Initial Teaching Alphabet, a phonetic spelling system consisting of 44 letters and code symbols designed to enable poor learners to read and write faster.

**Ives, Charles Edward**  1874–1954. Composer. Ives composed orchestral, choral, and chamber music marked by polytonal harmonies and unusual rhythms.

**Ives, James Merritt**  See CURRIER AND IVES.

**Ivy League**  a group of prestigious northeastern universities and colleges, so called because their buildings, constructed in an earlier era, were all ivy-covered. They include DARTMOUTH COLLEGE in NEW HAMPSHIRE, BROWN UNIVERSITY in RHODE ISLAND, YALE UNIVERSITY in CONNECTICUT, HARVARD UNIVERSITY in MASSACHUSETTS, CORNELL UNIVERSITY and COLUMBIA UNIVERSITY in NEW YORK, PRINCETON UNIVERSITY in NEW JERSEY, and the UNIVERSITY OF PENNSYLVANIA.

# J

**jackrabbit** a native North American hare with long ears and strong back legs.

**Jackson, Andrew** 1767–1845. Seventh president of the United States (1829–1837). His nickname was *Old Hickory*.

**Jackson, Mahalia** 1911–1972. Singer. Jackson helped to establish GOSPEL MUSIC as a distinct genre with her majestic contralto and commanding presence on the stage.

*jackrabbit*

**Jacuzzi** a trademarked name for a bath equipped with a device for swirling the water.

**jambalaya** a CAJUN dish of rice cooked with a mixture of ham, chicken, sausage, or shellfish, and seasoned with herbs.

**James, Henry, Jr.** 1843–1916. Author. Member of a distinguished NEW ENGLAND family, James is noted for existential novels such as *The Portrait of a Lady* (1881) and *The Wings of the Dove* (1902).

**James, Jesse** 1847–1882. Legendary outlaw. James, along with his brother Frank and the rest of his gang of outlaws, terrorized the central United States in the 1870s by robbing trains and banks. He was finally killed by one of his own men who sought the reward money offered for James's death. Exaggerated stories of James's exploits have made him a legendary figure.

**James, William** 1842–1910. Psychologist. Brother of novelist HENRY JAMES JR., William James pioneered in the study of psychology and established a strong reputation as a founder of the philosophy of pragmatism. Among his best known works are *The Principles of Psychology* (1890), *The Varieties of Religious Experience* (1902), and *Pragmatism* (1907).

**Jamestown** colony in VIRGINIA, the first permanent English settlement in North America, founded in 1607 under the leadership of Captain JOHN SMITH.

**Jane Crow** discrimination against women. Patterned on JIM CROW.

**Jane Doe** See JOHN DOE; JANE DOE.

**JAP** a Jewish-American Princess, a disparaging term used in reference to a wealthy young Jewish woman who expects to be pampered.

**jaws of life** a hydraulic device used in emergency rescue work shaped like a pair of scissors in which the jaws are used to pry things apart or lift them.

**Jay, John** 1745–1829. American statesman. Jay was president of the CONTINENTAL CONGRESS (1778) and the first chief justice of the SUPREME COURT.

**Jaycees** a business and civic organization founded in St. Louis, MISSOURI, in 1915 for young males. The name is a contraction of Junior Chamber of Commerce.

**Jayhawk State** KANSAS.

**jazz** an indigenous American musical form characterized by syncopation, improvisation, and rhythm, and incorporating elements from African music, RAGTIME, and BLUES. Originally played in the brothels of the Storyville redlight district in New Orleans, LOUISIANA, brass accompaniments were later added, creating the DIXIELAND style. The style was taken up by white musicians and transformed into dance music by the 1920s. Jazz led the way for the BIG BAND sound of the 1930s SWING music, and reached the peak of its popularity in the 1930s, with BENNY GOODMAN and DUKE ELLINGTON expanding the scope of jazz with innovative blends of solo and orchestra.

**Jazz Age** the era from 1920 to 1940, in which JAZZ music was highly popular. During this period, many people defied convention by ignoring PROHIBITION and by establishing new forms of dance, dress, and social behavior.

*Jeep*

**Jeep** a trademarked name for a four-wheel drive, all-terrain vehicle, originally designed for military transport. From general purpose, GP.

**Jefferson Memorial** a WASHINGTON, D.C. monument to THOMAS JEFFERSON. It is a columned building of white marble that contains a statue of Jefferson.

**Jefferson, Thomas** 1743–1826. Third president of the United States (1801–1809). Jefferson, a statesman and one of the FOUNDING FATHERS, drafted the DECLARATION OF INDEPENDENCE. He was also an accomplished architect and bibliophile, who helped to shape American culture in its formative years.

**Jehovah's Witness** a religious sect, with some Christian elements, founded in 1872 by Charles T. Russell (1852–1916), as a millenarian group. Among its tenets are rejection of blood transfusion, military service, and salute to national flags.

*Thomas Jefferson*

**Jesus Freaks** See JESUS PEOPLE.

**Jesus Movement** a Protestant Christian movement that draws young people, especially from the drug culture or the counterculture, to personally commit their lives to serving Jesus Christ, independently of any of the established churches or denominations.

**Jesus People** the collective name for committed Christians converted from the counterculture. Also known as *Jesus Freaks*.

**jet lag** a body clock disturbance resulting from traveling by jet across several time zones in a 12-hour period.

**jewel box** a plastic or cardboard container for CD-ROMs.

**Jewish Community Centers** institutions that provide physical education classes, day camps, arts classes, etc., to the Jewish community and promote cultural unity. The Young Men's Hebrew Association (YMHA) and Young Women's Hebrew Association (YWHA), established in the 1880s to serve Jewish youths, combined under the title of Jewish Community Centers to extend their services to the entire Jewish community. More than 400 centers exist in the United States and Canada.

**JFK** JOHN FITZGERALD KENNEDY.

**Jim Crow** 1. a pejorative name for AFRICAN-AMERICANS. 2. restrictive laws against AFRICAN-AMERICANS passed in the SOUTH after RECONSTRUCTION.

**jitterbug** a ballroom dance marked by fast footwork, turns, and acrobatics.

**job action** a form of labor protest short of a strike, generally a slowdown or work-to-rule.

**John Birch Society** an ultraconservative anticommunist group founded in 1958 by manufacturer Robert H. W. Welch (1899–1985). Named after John Birch, an American Baptist missionary who was killed by Communists in China in 1945.

**John Doe; Jane Doe** 1. a fictional name for an average American. 2. an unknown or unidentified person; the name used on official documents when a person's name is not known.

**john** a toilet (slang).

**Johnson, Andrew** 1808–1875. Seventeenth president of the United States (1865–1869).

**Johnson, Lyndon Baines** 1908–1973. Thirty-sixth president of the United States (1963–1969). Johnson introduced the GREAT SOCIETY reforms. Commonly known as LBJ.

**Johnson, Philip Cortelyou** 1906–. Architect. Johnson shaped architectural ideas as a critic, author, historian, and practicing architect. His buildings range from the International style to Classical and Post-Modernism, and include the Seagram Building, the New York State Theater at the Lincoln Center, the Boston Public Library's New Wing, Penzoil Place, and the AT&T Building.

**Jones, Edward D.** See DOW-JONES INDUSTRIAL AVERAGE.

**Joplin, Janis Lyn** 1943–1970. BLUES and ROCK AND ROLL singer. A rebel who exemplified the countercultural movement of the 1960s, Joplin was the archetypal HIPPIE and free spirit who transformed communal values into dynamic music performed with a frenzied energy that became her signature style.

*Janis Joplin*

**Joplin, Scott** 1868–1917. Ragtime composer, pianist. Known as the Father of RAGTIME, one of his best-known works is the "Maple Leaf Rag."

**judicare** a program for providing free legal services to the poor. Patterned on MEDICARE.

**jugate** a button showing two overlapping heads, such as those of a presidential candidate and his running mate.

**jukebox** a coin-operated record player originally installed in bars called *juke joints*.

*jukebox*

**jump cut** a sudden cut made in the middle of a continuous shot to show discontinuities in action.

**junk bond** a high-risk, high-return noncorporate bond bought at considerably less than face value.

**junk phone** phone lines beginning with a 900- AREA CODE offering a variety of services, some of them considered questionable.

**K of C** KNIGHTS OF COLUMBUS.

**Kahn, Louis Isadore** 1901–1974. Architect. A legend in his own lifetime, Kahn was one of the most powerful influences in architecture as a teacher, theorist, and practitioner. His innovations extended not only to structure but to materials and volume. His most memorable buildings include the UNIVERSITY OF PENNSYLVANIA Medical Research Building, La Jolla Salk Institute, Phillips Exeter Academy, Fort Worth Kimball Art Museum, and the Yale Center for British Art and Studies.

**Kansas** a state in the U.S. MIDWEST. Known as the Sunflower State or the Jayhawk State, its capital is Topeka, and Wichita is its largest city. The western meadowlark is the state bird of Kansas, and the sunflower is its state flower.

**karaoke** a device that enables a singer to be accompanied by prerecorded music.

**Kaufman, George S.** 1889–1961. Playwright. Kaufman collaborated with Moss Hart (1904–1961) on a number of successful BROADWAY plays, especially, *You Can't Take It with You* (1936) and *The Man Who Came to Dinner* (1939).

**Keaton, Buster** 1895–1966. Film actor, director, and producer, comedian and mime. Considered the equal of CHARLIE CHAPLIN, Keaton specialized in drawing laughter out of disasters and accidents.

**keelboat** a shallow-draft riverboat used for hauling freight on the MISSISSIPPI RIVER.

**Keller, Helen Adams** 1880–1968. Lecturer, author, social activist for the disabled. Blind and deaf from infancy, Keller overcame her odds and wrote a number of books, including *The Story of My Life* (1903).

**Kennedy, John Fitzgerald** 1917–1963. Thirty-fifth president of the United States (1961–1963). Kennedy was the youngest man to be elected president and the first Roman Catholic to hold the office. Commonly referred to as JFK, he was assassinated in 1963, allegedly by LEE HARVEY OSWALD. See also CAMELOT; NEW FRONTIER; ONASSIS, JACKIE; PEACE CORPS.

**Kentucky** a state in the east-central United States. Kentucky is called the Bluegrass State. Its capital is Frankfort and its largest city is Louisville. The cardinal is the state bird, and the state flower is the goldenrod.

**Kentucky colonel** a person commissioned as an honorary colonel by the State of KENTUCKY. The commission has no military significance.

**Kentucky Derby** a horse race run since 1875 on the first Saturday in May at Churchill Downs racetrack in Louisville, KENTUCKY.

**Kentucky Revival** the GREAT REVIVAL.

**Keogh plan** any of various plans by which self-employed individuals may set aside up to 15 percent of their annual income as a tax-deferred annuity or retirement fund.

**Kern, Jerome David** 1885–1945. Composer. Creator of the BROADWAY musical, Kern wrote songs for over 100 stage productions, including the most famous of them all, *Showboat* (1927).

**Kerouac, Jack** 1922–1969. Writer. Kerouac was a leading member of the BEAT GENERATION. His 1957 novel, *On the Road*, was its defining manifesto.

**Kevorkian, Dr. Jack** a pioneer in physician-assisted suicide, Kevorkian was arrested several times in the 1990s for helping terminally ill patients end their lives. He is nicknamed *Dr. Death*.

**Kewpie doll** a small, chubby doll made since 1913 modeled on figures created by Rose O'Neill (1874–1944).

**Key West** one of the FLORIDA KEYS, and also a city on the island of Key West.

**keyboard** to enter information or data into a computer by means of a keyboard.

**Keynesianism** See DEMAND-SIDE.

**Keystone Kops** blundering policemen in silent-film comedies created by the Keystone Company. Their chases of the wrong suspects generally ended in incredible foul-ups.

**Keystone State** PENNSYLVANIA.

**kidvid** children's television programs or videotapes.

**King, B. B.** 1925–. BLUES musician and guitarist, born Riley B. King.

**King, Martin Luther, Jr.** 1929–1968. Civil rights leader. King struggled to end discrimination against AFRICAN-AMERICANS and to win them political and civil equality with other races. He led the March on WASHINGTON, D.C. in 1963, where he delivered his famous "I Have a Dream" speech. He received the Nobel Prize for Peace in 1964. King was assassinated in 1968.

*Martin Luther King, Jr.*

**King Ranch** a huge TEXAS cattle ranch, estimated to cover half a million acres over five counties. It was founded by Richard King (1825–1885).

**King, The** 1. ELVIS PRESLEY. 2. CLARK GABLE.

**Kingfish** nickname of HUEY LONG.

**Kinsey, Alfred Charles** 1894–1956. Scientist in sexology. His Kinsey Report applied scientific techniques to the study of sexual behavior.

**kiss and tell** a book or article which reveals titillating personal secrets of the writer's friends and lovers.

**Kitty Hawk** a NORTH CAROLINA town, site of the first powered airplane flight by the WRIGHT BROTHERS.

**Kiwanis International** a philanthropic business and community service organization founded in 1915 in Detroit.

**Klan** the KU KLUX KLAN.

**klieg light** a powerful carbon arc lamp producing an intense light, used primarily in filmmaking. It is named after the brothers John H. and Anton T. Kliegl, German-born U.S. inventors.

**Klondike gold rush** the rush of thousands of U.S. citizens to the Klondike region of Canada in the late 1890s after gold was discovered there in 1896.

**kneeling bus** a bus with a pneumatic suspension system that enables it to lower its body to the level of the curb, a feature specially designed to help handicapped people.

**Knickerbocker** 1. pseudonym of WASHINGTON IRVING, author of *A History of New York* (1809). 2. a New Yorker.

**Knights of Columbus** a Roman Catholic fraternal organization founded in New Haven, CONNECTICUT, in 1882. Sometimes abbreviated K of C.

**Knox, George** a legendary lumberjack of the MAINE woods credited with prodigious feats of strength.

**Korean War** 1950–1953 conflict between the United Nations and communist North Korea that started when North Korea invaded South Korea. Most of the troops sent by the United Nations to aid the South Koreans were from the United States. In 1953, both sides signed a truce to end the fighting.

**KS** KANSAS. (The official two-letter post office abbreviation.)

**Ku Klux Klan** a white supremacist organization founded in TENNESSEE in 1865 to intimidate blacks from breaking the segregation barriers erected against them after the RECONSTRUCTION. To add to their terror tactics, members of the Klan wore

*members of the Ku Klux Klan*

ghostlike robes and hoods and burned large wooden crosses, usually during the night, as an expression of their anger. Sometimes called *night riders.*

**Kuznets, Simon Smith** 1901–1985. Economist. Kuznets was a pioneer in national income accounting who developed the macroeconomic system by which the gross national product (GNP) is calculated. Awarded the Nobel Prize in Economic Sciences in 1971.

**Kwanza** an AFRICAN-AMERICAN festival held in late December.

**KY** KENTUCKY. (The official two-letter post office abbreviation.)

# L

**LA**  Louisiana. (The official two-letter post office abbreviation.)

**La Guardia, Fiorello**  1882–1947. Politician. La Guardia was mayor of New York City from 1933 to 1945. He was nicknamed the Little Flower.

**Labor Day**  the first Monday in September, celebrated since 1894 as a national holiday honoring workers. It also marks the unofficial end of summer and the beginning of fall.

**Lake Erie**  the shallowest of the Great Lakes, it touches the states of New York, Pennsylvania, Ohio, and Michigan.

**Lake Huron**  one of the Great Lakes, it is bounded on the west by Michigan and on the north and east by Ontario, Canada.

**Lake Mead**  a reservoir in the Colorado River created by the Hoover Dam.

**Lake Michigan**  one of the Great Lakes, it touches the states of Michigan, Illinois, Indiana, and Wisconsin.

**Lake of the Ozarks**  a large manmade lake in Missouri.

**Lake Ontario**  the smallest of the Great Lakes, it touches Ontario, Canada and New York.

**Lake Superior**  the largest of the Great Lakes, it touches Minnesota, Wisconsin, Michigan, and Ontario, Canada.

**Lamaze**  a form of natural childbirth based on Pavlov's studies of the conditioned reflex, developed by the French obstetrician, Fernand Lamaze.

**LAN** local area network, which links a group of computers and printers together.

**Land of Enchantment** NEW MEXICO.

**Land of Lincoln** ILLINOIS.

**Land of Opportunity** ARKANSAS.

**Land of 10,000 Lakes** MINNESOTA.

**Land of the Midnight Sun** ALASKA.

**landfill** 1. garbage and other wastes that are disposed of by being deposited into the earth. 2. a deposit of garbage and other wastes in the earth. 3. to dispose of garbage and other wastes by depositing them in the earth.

**Lardner, Ring(gold Wilmer)** 1885–1933. Writer and humorist. Lardner was among the first to use common spoken language in short stories and fiction and to reveal what was beneath the surface of ordinary life.

**Las Vegas** a NEVADA city with many casinos, known as the gambling capital of the United States.

**Las Vegas Night** a legal gambling event conducted by a nonprofit organization, such as a church or synagogue, to raise money for its philanthropic activities.

**Last Frontier** ALASKA.

**last hurrah** a final or farewell act or effort at the end of a long career. From the title of a novel about Boston mayor James M. Curley (1874–1958), by Edwin O'Connor (1918–1968).

**latchkey child** a child left unsupervised for part of the day at a locked home when the parents are away at work.

**lateral thinking** exploratory thinking that emphasizes breadth and range rather than details.

**Latino** a Latin American; a Hispanic.

**Latrobe, Benjamin Henry** 1764–1820. Architect. The first architect of international renown in U.S. history, Latrobe was commissioned in 1803 to build the CAPITOL. Among his other notable buildings are the Baltimore Roman Catholic Cathedral, Christ Church and St. John's Church in WASHINGTON, D.C., and the Baltimore Stock Exchange.

**Latter-day Saints, Church of Jesus Christ of**  the official name of the MORMON church, a denomination founded by JOSEPH SMITH.

**launder**  to channel illegal money through a bank or other legitimate enterprise to give it the appearance of legitimacy and escape official scrutiny.

**Laurel and Hardy**  a successful HOLLYWOOD comedy team of the 1930s, partnering comedians Stan Laurel (1890–1965) and Oliver Hardy (1892–1957).

**lavalier**  a very small microphone hung around the neck or clipped to the lapel of a speaker or singer.

**LBJ**  LYNDON BAINES JOHNSON.

**leading indicators**  key indicators which reflect the pace of economic growth and on which lesser indicators are based.

**League of Women Voters**  a nonpartisan women's group organized in 1920 to encourage political education and informed involvement in government. Abbreviated LWV.

**learning curve**  a hypothetical curve that displays the pace of adaptation or acquisition of skills relative to the practical difficulties encountered by the learner.

**leatherneck**  a nickname for a member of the U.S. Marine Corps.

***Leaves of Grass***  WALT WHITMAN's book of poems first published in 1855 and expanded continuously until the final version was published in 1892. It revolutionized poetic style in America.

**Lee, Robert E.**  1807–1870. CONFEDERATE general. Lee, considered a military genius, led the Confederate forces during the CIVIL WAR.

**Left Coast**  the west coast of the United States.

**lei**  in HAWAII, a garland or wreath of flowers.

**Lerner and Loewe** a musical-comedy writing team, partnering lyricist Alan Jay Lerner (1918–1986) and composer Frederick Loewe (1904–1988). Their greatest success was *My Fair Lady* (1956).

**level playing field** a state of equality that ensures no contestant has undue advantage or privilege and the competition is fair and open.

**leveraged buyout** the purchase of a corporation by a group of investors largely through money borrowed from banks to be paid back from future profits.

**Levis** Trademark. Blue denim jeans, originally made for CALIFORNIA miners by Levi Strauss and Company.

**Lewis and Clark Expedition** the expedition to survey the LOUISIANA PURCHASE and to find the Northwest Passage, commissioned by THOMAS JEFFERSON in 1803. It was led by Jefferson's private secretary, Meriwether Lewis (1774–1809) and army officer William Clark (1770–1838).

**Lewis, Sinclair** 1885–1951. Novelist. In 1930 Lewis became the first American to win the Nobel Prize for Literature. He developed a new genre of satire to ridicule Main Street American values and capitalism. Among his best-known works are *Main Street* (1920), *Babbitt* (1922), *Arrowsmith* (1925), and *Elmer Gantry* (1927).

**Lewis, John Llewellyn** 1880–1969. Labor leader. A controversial figure, Lewis founded the Congress of Industrial Organizations (see AFL-CIO) and made it one of the most important labor organizations. He was president of the United Mine Workers from 1920 to 1960.

**Liberty Bell** a cast-iron bell, weighing over a ton, that originally hung in INDEPENDENCE HALL,

*Liberty Bell*

Philadelphia, and is now a major tourist attraction in a pavillion on the same site. Its most famous feature is a vertical crack. It rang in honor of both the signing of the DECLARATION OF INDEPENDENCE and the Yorktown surrender.

**Library of Congress** the national library of the United States and the official copyright depository. It was established in 1800.

**Lichtenstein, Roy** 1923–. Painter. He cofounded the POP ART movement with ANDY WARHOL and became one of its prime practitioners.

*Life* a pioneering photo magazine founded in 1935 by publisher HENRY LUCE.

**lifeboat ethics** ethical guidelines in a catastrophic emergency that postulate the survival of only the most useful without reference to humanitarian or moral principles and that assign priorities according to expediency. Compare TRIAGE.

**life-support system** mechanical medical devices designed to keep a person alive in life-threatening situations.

**limousine liberal** a wealthy person who espouses liberal or left-wing causes.

**Lincoln, Abraham** 1809–1865. Sixteenth president of the United States (1861–1865). Born in a Kentucky LOG CABIN, Lincoln received little formal schooling and was largely self-taught. He was a partner in a successful law practice in ILLINOIS before entering the world of politics. As president, Lincoln led the UNION in the CIVIL WAR, issued the EMANCIPATION PROCLAMATION, and delivered the famous GETTYSBURG

*Abraham Lincoln*

Address. He was assassinated at Ford's Theatre in 1865 by John Wilkes Booth.

**Lincoln Memorial** a monument in Washington Mall that resembles a Greek Temple and contains a large statue of Abraham Lincoln. It was dedicated in 1922.

**Lindbergh, Charles** 1902–1974. Aviator. Lindbergh, in his monoplane called *The Spirit of St. Louis*, was the first to fly solo and nonstop across the Atlantic. He became a celebrated hero and was nicknamed the Lone Eagle and Lucky Lindy. The kidnapping and murder of his infant son in 1932 made news around the world. Later in life, Lindbergh became a strong isolationist and environmentalist.

**Lindsay, Vachel** 1879–1931. Poet and wandering minstrel. His most famous work, *General William Booth Enters into Heaven* (1913) was a tribute to the founder of the Salvation Army.

**Lippmann, Walter** 1889–1974. Political commentator and journalist. Lippmann was an influential pundit whose syndicated column appeared in more than 200 newspapers with nearly 40 million readers. He founded the *New Republic* in 1914.

**Little Bighorn, Battle of the** 1876 battle at the Little Bighorn River in Montana between General George Armstrong Custer's cavalry unit and Native Americans. Custer underestimated the Native American forces, which consisted of the Sioux, led by Chief Sitting Bull, the Cheyenne, and others. Custer and all of his men were killed.

**Little Flower** Fiorello La Guardia.

**Little Italy** the section of a large town populated mostly by Italians.

**living will** a will that spells out a person's intentions regarding medical treatment, burial, etc., in case he or she is incapacitated.

**lockstep** a rigid and inflexible arrangement.

**log cabin** a type of dwelling, common in the frontier settlements in the 19th century, made of rough-hewn notched logs

*log cabin*

with caulking made of dirt. Five U.S. presidents were born in log cabins: ANDREW JACKSON, JAMES POLK, JAMES BUCHANAN, ABRAHAM LINCOLN, and JAMES GARFIELD.

**log rolling** in politics, to trade favors or votes for favors or votes in return.

**London, Jack** 1876–1916. Writer. London is best known for his Klondike stories, especially *The Call of the Wild* (1903), which portrayed human struggle against natural and social adversities.

**Lone Eagle, the** CHARLES LINDBERGH.

**Lone Star State** TEXAS. The flag of the Republic of Texas (1836–1846) had a single star.

**lonelyhearts column** an advice column in newspapers and magazines for lovelorn persons.

**Long, Huey** 1893–1935. Politician. Long, considered a ruthless demagogue, was governor of LOUISIANA from 1928–1932. He was assassinated in 1935.

**Longfellow, Henry Wadsworth** 1807–1882. Poet. Longfellow was the most famous poet of the 19th century, popular on both sides of the Atlantic. Among his best-known poems are *The Village Blacksmith* (1841), *The Wreck of the Hesperus* (1841), *Evangeline* (1847), and *Song of Hiawatha* (1855).

**longhorn cattle** TEXAS LONGHORN.

**Los Angelization** explosive and uncontrolled growth of a city resulting in pollution, land damage, overcrowding, poor social services, traffic congestion, and violent crime. From Los Angeles, CALIFORNIA, which grew fast in recent decades to overtake Chicago, ILLINOIS, as the second largest U.S. city.

**Lost Cause** the cause of the CONFEDERACY in the CIVIL WAR.

**Lost Colony** See ROANOKE COLONY.

**Lost Generation** a term coined by GERTRUDE STEIN to describe the rootless and disillusioned generation of artists and writers that emerged from WORLD WAR I and the interwar years.

**Louis, Joe** 1914–1981. Boxer. Nicknamed the Brown Bomber, Louis was the heavyweight champion for 12 years.

**Louisiana** a state in the southeastern United States. Its capital is Baton Rouge and New Orleans is its largest city. Called the Pelican State, its state bird is the pelican and its state flower is the magnolia. Abbreviated LA.

**Louisiana Purchase** the $15 million purchase in 1803 by the United States from France of French territory between the MISSISSIPPI RIVER and the ROCKY MOUNTAINS.

**love bombing** the display of contrived affection and respect toward a new convert by members of a cult.

**Lowell, James Russell** 1819–1891. Poet and author. Lowell was the first editor of the *ATLANTIC MONTHLY* and a fervent abolitionist.

**Lowell, Robert Traill Spence, Jr.** 1917–1977. Poet. Scion of a noted NEW ENGLAND literary family, Lowell's confessional poetry, especially *Life Studies* (1959), changed the course of American poetry.

**lower forty-eight** the 48 contiguous U.S. states south of Canada.

**Loyalist** an American colonist who was passively or actively opposed to the REVOLUTIONARY WAR and secession from Great Britain. Also called a TORY.

**luau** in HAWAII, a public feast.

**Luce, Henry** 1898–1967. Editor and publisher. Founder of *Time, Life, Fortune*, and other mass-circulation magazines, Luce was one of the most successful media barons of the 20th century.

**Lucky Lindy** CHARLES LINDBERGH.

**luddite** a person who is hostile to the growing dominance of technology in modern life and who feels threatened by its ability to render certain types of work obsolete.

**lunch meat** spiced ground meat packed into a casing and cut in slices. See also COLD CUT.

**LWV** LEAGUE OF WOMEN VOTERS.

**lynching** extralegal punishment, including execution, meted out to criminals or racial minorities by vigilante groups.

**lynx** one of a number of American wild cats characterized by long legs, a short tail, and tufted ears.

**M or (M1)** money supply consisting of currency and demand deposits.

**M.A.** Master of Arts.

**MA** Massachusetts. (The official two-letter post office abbreviation.)

**Ma Bell** nickname for Bell Telephone Company.

**macarena** a lively dance of Hispanic origin performed in groups.

**MacGuffin** term coined by Alfred Hitchcock for a seemingly minor element around which a suspense story revolves or which prefigures the ending.

**machine language** the coding system that processes information in a computer.

**MacLeish, Archibald** 1892–1982. Poet. MacLeish was also a committed public servant as the Librarian of Congress under Franklin Delano Roosevelt, and a founder of UNESCO (United Nations Educational, Scientific, and Cultural Organization). His best-known verse play is *J.B.* (1958).

**Mad Anthony** 1745–1796. Anthony Wayne, one of the military heroes of the Revolutionary War, noted for his savagery.

**MADD** Mothers Against Drunk Driving. A group dedicated to preventing drunk-driving deaths by educating people, especially students, about the dangers of driving while intoxicated.

**Madison Avenue** the advertising industry. From Madison Avenue in New York City, where the major advertising firms are located.

**Madison, James** 1751–1836. Fourth president of the United States (1809–1817). As a member of the CONSTITUTIONAL CONVENTION, Madison played a major role in the development of the CONSTITUTION.

**Madison Square Garden** a major sports arena in MANHATTAN.

**Mafia** a secret criminal organization believed to be of Sicilian origin. Also known as *the Mob* and Cosa Nostra ("our thing"), it is the largest organized crime syndicate in the United States.

**magalog** a catalog enriched with articles and photographs of a general nature; a blend of catalog and magazine.

**magic bullet** a miracle drug that can heal a killer disease or halt its spread in a way that defies explanation.

**Magic Kingdom, the** one of the three major parks that make up WALT DISNEY WORLD, located near Orlando, FLORIDA.

**Magic Marker** Trademark. A pen used for marking or drawing that has a felt tip and a metal container holding quick-drying, waterproof ink.

**Magnolia State** MISSISSIPPI.

**mail bomb** an explosive device hidden in a letter or parcel designed to detonate when opened.

**Mailer, Norman Kingsley** 1923–. Novelist. Mailer is an iconoclastic writer who achieved extraordinary fame with his first novel, *The Naked and the Dead* (1948), based on his experiences in WORLD WAR II.

**Main Street** conventional or mainstream. From SINCLAIR LEWIS's novel of the same name, portraying a dull town.

**Maine** a state in the northeastern United States. Maine's capital is Augusta, and Portland is its largest city. Called the Pine Tree State, its state flower is the white pine cone and tassel, and its state bird is the chickadee. Abbreviated ME.

**mainframe** the central processor of a computer network.

**Malamud, Bernard** 1914–1986. Writer. Malamud introduced Jewish themes into modern American fiction, as in his 1957 novel, *The Assistant*.

**Malcolm X** 1925–1965. Black revolutionary. Born Malcolm Little, he changed his name upon joining the NATION OF ISLAM in the 1950s. He was assassinated by a rival Muslim faction.

**mall** a large group of stores, often completely enclosed in a building. In addition to stores, many malls contain restaurants, banks, and movie theaters. Also called a *shopping mall* or a *shopping center*.

**mall rat** an adolescent who spends most of his or her free time hanging out in a MALL.

*Malcolm X*

**Mall, The** WASHINGTON MALL.

**Mammoth Cave** a large cave in southern KENTUCKY that is a popular tourist attraction. The cave has many chambers, a few limestone formations, and lakes and rivers, and was originally inhabited by NATIVE AMERICANS. The surrounding area is a national park.

**Manhattan** a borough of New York City that is its commercial and cultural center.

**Manhattan Project** a secret U.S. government project during WORLD WAR II that produced the atomic bomb in 1945.

**manifest destiny** the philosophical basis for American imperialist ambitions. It rationalizes imperialist expansion as preordained or inevitable. The term was coined by journalist John O'Sullivan

(1813–1895), who used it in an editorial to call for the annexation of TEXAS.

**Mann Act** an act passed by the U.S. CONGRESS in 1910 prohibiting the interstate transport of females for immoral purposes. Also called the White Slave Traffic Act.

**Mann, Horace** 1796–1859. Educator. Pioneer, known as the Father of Public Education, Mann helped to establish public education as a citizen's right, and is credited with creating the first teachers' schools, winning higher salaries for teachers, and organizing annual educational conventions.

**Mapplethorpe, Robert** 1946–1989. Photographer. Many of Mapplethorpe's austere black and white photographs were designed to shock the bourgeoisie with their frankly erotic content.

**marathon** any of several long-distance footraces held in cities, generally of 26 miles and 385 yards. From Marathon in ancient Greece, site of a famous Greek victory over the Persians, news of which was carried to Athens, 26 miles and 385 yards away, by a runner.

**March of Time** a weekly newsreel produced by Time, Inc., and shown in movie theaters from 1935 to 1961.

**Mardi Gras** a pre-Lenten carnival period, celebrated especially in New Orleans, LOUISIANA, marked by parades and drunken revels.

**marginalize** to exclude from active participation by ignoring or by minimizing importance.

*Mardi Gras parade*

**mariachi** a Mexican band featuring guitars, violins, and brass instruments, originally employed at weddings.

**Marshall, John** 1755–1835. Jurist. The first great chief justice of the United States, Marshall dominated the SUPREME COURT from 1801 to

1835, establishing basic constitutional and judicial principles and concepts, such as judicial review and implied powers.

**Marshall Plan** a massive U.S. aid program for rebuilding Europe and containing the spread of Communism, named after George Marshall (1880–1959), the secretary of state who introduced it in 1947.

**Marx Brothers** Five comedians—Julius Henry (1890–1977), Leonard (1891–1961), Arthur (1893–1964), Milton (1894–1977), and Herbert (1901–1979), who performed under the names Groucho, Chico, Harpo, Gummo, and Zeppo—who made slapstick into an art form. They made several successful HOLLYWOOD comedies in the 1930s.

**Maryland** a state in the eastern United States. Known as the Free State or the Old Line State, its capital is Annapolis, and its largest city is Baltimore. The Baltimore oriole is Maryland's state bird and the black-eyed Susan is its state flower. Abbreviated MD.

**MASH** mobile army surgical hospital. A movable hospital base used to treat soldiers injured in combat during war.

**Mason-Dixon Line** the symbolic border between NORTH and SOUTH, demarcated between PENNSYLVANIA and MARYLAND in the 1760s by British surveyors Charles Mason and Jeremiah Dixon.

**Massachusetts** a state in the northeastern United States. Boston is both the capital and the largest city of Massachusetts. Massachusetts is known as the Bay State or the Old Colony State. Its state flower is the mayflower, and its state bird is the chickadee. Abbreviated MA.

**Master of Arts** a postgraduate degree ranking above BACHELOR OF ARTS and beneath the doctorate. It is awarded to a graduate student who has finished a designated course of study in an area of the humanities. Abbreviated M.A.

**Master of Science** a postgraduate degree ranking above BACHELOR OF SCIENCE and beneath the doctorate. It is awarded to a graduate student who has finished a designated course of study in an area of the sciences. Abbreviated M.S.

**Mather, Cotton** 1663–1728. PURITAN clergyman. Son of Increase Mather (1639–1723), Cotton Mather was a third-generation Puritan

## Mauldin, Bill

pastor who helped to define the Puritan faith and practice. He was also a prolific writer who wrote more than 100 books and pamphlets in his lifetime.

**Mauldin, Bill**  1921–. Cartoonist. During WORLD WAR II, Mauldin worked on the staff of the U.S. Army newspaper, *Stars and Stripes*.

**maven**  an expert or connoisseur. From Hebrew *mevin*.

**maverick**  a person who refuses to accept party discipline or follow party dictates but insists on doing as he or she pleases. From Samuel A. Maverick, 1803–1870, a TEXAS cattle owner who refused to brand his cattle.

**Mayflower**  the ship that carried the first permanent settlers of NEW ENGLAND from Europe to America. It sailed from Plymouth, England, in September 1620 and after a two-month voyage reached MASSACHUSETTS, where its passengers, the PILGRIMS, established the PLYMOUTH COLONY.

**McCarthy era**  a period in the 1950s when MCCARTHYISM was practiced.

**McCarthy, Mary Therese**  1912–1989. Writer. McCarthy was a controversial writer who wrote on a wide range of subjects and personalities. She is best noted for *The Group* (1963), a chronicle of the experiences of eight young graduates of Vassar College.

**McCarthyism**  an anticommunist witch hunt conducted by Senator Joseph McCarthy (1908–1957) between 1953 and 1954.

**McCoy, the real**  See REAL MCCOY, THE.

**McGready, James**  See GREAT REVIVAL.

**McGuffey Readers**  a series of grade school texts written by educator William Holmes McGuffey (1800–1873). They formed the basic curriculum of most elementary schools in the 19th-century United States.

**McKinley, William**  1843–1901. Twenty-fifth president of the United States (1897–1901). McKinley was assassinated in office. MOUNT MCKINLEY bears his name.

**McLuhanism** the ideas of Canadian writer, Marshall McLuhan (1911–1980), who forecast the impact of television and electronic communications on future society and coined the term GLOBAL VILLAGE.

**M.D.** *Medicinae Doctor*, Latin for Doctor of Medicine. The graduate degree awarded to a student who has successfully completed a predetermined course of study in medicine.

**MD** MARYLAND. (The official two-letter post office abbreviation.)

**MDT** MOUNTAIN DAYLIGHT TIME.

**ME** MAINE. (The official two-letter post office abbreviation.)

**Mead, Margaret** 1901–1978. Anthropologist. Mead was curator of ethnology at the American Museum of Natural History in New York City from 1964 to 1969. A disciple of FRANZ BOAS, she is best remembered as the writer of *Coming of Age in Samoa* (1928), a seminal work in anthropology.

**Meany, George** 1894–1980. Labor leader. Meany was president of the AFL-CIO from 1955 to 1980. A staunch anticommunist, he was also a tough bargainer.

**meat loaf** one or more types of ground meat with spices and other ingredients, molded into the shape of a loaf and baked.

**medevac** to carry people in dire emergencies to a hospital by helicopter. From medical evacuation.

**media event** an event deliberately staged in order to attract extensive media coverage.

**Medicaid** a government health insurance program for the poor, financed by the federal government and the states.

**Medicare** a government health insurance program introduced in 1965 that provides medical care to the elderly. It is financed by government funds and SOCIAL SECURITY payments.

**Megan's Law** a law requiring convicted pedophiles and child molesters to report to the police of the communities where they reside after their release from jail.

**Meier, Richard Alan**  1934–. Architect. Meier developed his architectural ideas stressing balance between light, form, and space, and created elegant buildings. Among his notable buildings are the Atheneum in INDIANA (1979), Atlanta's High Musuem of Art (1983), and Douglas House in MICHIGAN (1973).

**meltdown**  1. the melting, due to malfunction or accident, of the fuel core of a nuclear reactor. 2. the disastrous breakdown of any system or mechanism.

**melting pot**  a term coined by English author Israel Zangwill describing America as a crucible where the various immigrant cultures are melded and their value systems and social structures are homogenized.

**Melville, Herman**  1819–1891. Novelist. He is best known as the author of *Moby Dick* (1851), an eerie story of a whaler's pursuit of a white whale.

**Memorial Day**  a national holiday honoring the war dead, celebrated on the last Monday in May. It was originally called Decoration Day and marks the unofficial beginning of summer.

**Mencken, H. L.**  1880–1956. Critic and journalist. An iconoclast who mercilessly skewered religious and social hypocrisy and foibles, Mencken also was a philologist whose *The American Language* remains a classic. He was founder and editor (with GEORGE JEAN NATHAN) of *The American Mercury*, introduced in 1924.

**Mensa**  an association of persons with an IQ score higher than that of 98 percent of the population.

**menu**  any list of programs or choices, especially as presented on a computer screen.

**merchant of death**  a trader in weapons of warfare, especially one who buys and sells guns, ammunition, and weaponry.

**Merman, Ethel**  1909–1984. Actress, singer. Merman introduced many songs by GEORGE GERSHWIN, IRVING BERLIN, and STEPHEN SONDHEIM in BROADWAY musicals.

**mesquite**  a spiny shrub that grows in the SONORAN DESERT and other parts of the southwestern United States. Its seeds, or beans, can be eaten, and its wood is now very popular for use in grilling meat.

**Met** the METROPOLITAN OPERA.

**Method, the** an acting technique developed by Russian director Konstantin Stanislavsky, involving intense identification of the actor with the character.

**Metroliner** a high-speed train on the AMTRAK railroad.

**Metropolitan Opera** the premier opera company of the United States, located in New York City. Often called the Met.

**Mexican War** a war fought from 1846 to 1848 between the United States and Mexico over possession of TEXAS. The victorious United States gained an enormous piece of land from Mexico, covering the present-day states of TEXAS, CALIFORNIA, NEVADA, and UTAH, and parts of ARIZONA, COLORADO, NEW MEXICO, and WYOMING.

**MGM** Metro-Goldwyn-Mayer; a major motion-picture production company.

**MI** MICHIGAN. (The official two-letter post office abbreviation.)

**MIA** missing in action, designating a missing combat soldier not reported as killed in action or taken as prisoner by the enemy.

**Michigan** a state of the U.S. MIDWEST. Called the Wolverine State, its capital is Lansing and its largest city is Detroit. The robin is Michigan's state bird, and the apple blossom is its state flower. Abbreviated MI.

**Mickey Mouse** 1. an animated character introduced by WALT DISNEY in 1928. 2. anything trivial or unimportant or too easy or simple to be concerned about.

**microbrewery** a small brewery on the premises of a restaurant or bar where the brewed product is sold.

**Middle America** a broad cross section of America representing mainstream values and holding middle-of-the-road positions on political issues.

**middle passage**  the transatlantic crossing of black slaves, as distinguished from their first passage from their homes to the slave ships and final passage from the U.S. port to the owners' homes.

**Midwest**  a section of the United States that includes the following states: ILLINOIS, INDIANA, IOWA, KANSAS, MICHIGAN, MINNESOTA, MISSOURI, NEBRASKA, OHIO, and WISCONSIN. The Midwest is noted for its agriculture and the GREAT LAKES.

**Mies van der Rohe, Ludwig**  1886–1969. Architect. With FRANK LLOYD WRIGHT and Swiss architect Corbusier, the German-born Mies was one of the three most influential architects of the 20th century, who developed the International Style. Among his most enduring legacies are the German Pavilion in Barcelona (1929) and the Seagram Building (1958).

**militia**  any right-wing, paramilitary, generally clandestine organization opposing established authority and dedicated to its overthrow.

**milk shake**  a cold drink made from milk, ice cream, and flavorings that is shaken or mixed in a blender.

**Millay, Edna St. Vincent**  1892–1950. Poet. Millay's lively poetic voice is best expressed in the collection *The Ballad of the Harp Weaver* (1923).

**Miller, Arthur**  1915–. Playwright. Miller's *Death of a Salesman* (1949) is one of the all-time classic plays of the American theater.

**Miller, Henry**  1891–1980. Writer. Miller took bold sensual themes as his subjects in his novels, particularly in *Tropic of Cancer* (1934) and *Tropic of Capricorn* (1939). He also wrote the classic travelogue *Colossus of Maroussi* (1941).

**Milquetoast**  a timid wimp, from Caspar Milquetoast, a comic-strip character in the late 1930s.

**Minnesota**  a state in the U.S. MIDWEST. Minnesota is known as the North Star State, the Gopher State, and the Land of 10,000 Lakes. Its capital is St. Paul, and its largest city is Minneapolis. The state bird is the common loon, and the state flower is the showy lady slipper. Abbreviated MN.

**minstrel show**  a 19th-century theater form in which whites blacked their faces and acted the roles of blacks, performing skits and songs with exaggerated NEGRO accents.

**mint julep**  a cold alcoholic drink made with whiskey, sugar, ice, and mint, popular in the SOUTH.

**Minutemen**  volunteer Colonial soldiers who could assemble at a moment's notice, ready to fight.

**Miranda Warning**  a law requiring police arresting a person to inform him or her of the civil rights of an accused, especially the right to remain silent and to have an attorney present during interrogation. From a SUPREME COURT ruling in the case of *Miranda v. Arizona*, 1966.

**Mississippi**  a state in the southern United States. The state capital and largest city is Jackson. Called the Magnolia State, its state flower is the magnolia and its state bird is the mockingbird. Abbreviated MS.

**Mississippi River**  the longest river in the United States, 2,350 miles long. It rises from MINNESOTA and flows south into the Gulf of Mexico. It has been nicknamed Big Muddy (for its muddy-colored water), Old Man River, and Father of Waters.

**Missouri**  a state in the central United States. Known as the Show-Me State, its largest city is St. Louis and its capital is Jefferson City. The bluebird is the state bird, and the hawthorne is the state flower. Abbreviated MO.

**Missouri River**  the second-longest river in the United States, rising in MONTANA and joining the MISSISSIPPI RIVER near St. Louis, MISSOURI. It is 2,315 miles long.

**MN**  MINNESOTA. (The official two-letter post office abbreviation.)

**MO**  MISSOURI. (The official two-letter post office abbreviation.)

**Mob, the**  the MAFIA.

**Moby Dick**  the great white whale appearing in the novel of the same name. See HERMAN MELVILLE.

**moccasin** NATIVE AMERICAN footwear made of deerskin with elaborate quillwork.

**Model T** an automobile that was mass-produced by the Ford Motor Company from 1909 to 1927. It dominated the automobile market until the mid-1920s.

*Model T*

**Mohawk** a NATIVE AMERICAN tribe, one of the members of the IROQUOIS LEAGUE. Many Mohawks fled America for Canada after the REVOLUTIONARY WAR.

**Mojave Desert** an arid area in southern CALIFORNIA that consists of barren mountains and flat valleys. It includes DEATH VALLEY.

**mole** 1. a machine that bores holes through rock, making tunnels. 2. a double agent or a member of a secret service who is actually working for a foreign espionage organization.

**Molly Maguires** an Irish-American secret society of Irish miners who opposed the mine owners in the 1860s and 1870s, using violent tactics as well as organized strikes.

**MOMA** MUSEUM OF MODERN ART.

**mom-and-pop store** a small business run by a husband-and-wife team.

**moment of truth** the decisive moment when a challenge one has been evading for a time must be faced without flinching.

**mommy track** a career break faced by women who place their corporate advancement on hold in order to have babies or devote more time to raising them.

**money market fund** a mutual fund specializing in investments in short-term instruments of credit.

**Monk, Thelonius** 1920–1982. Jazz musician. Monk's stripped-down compositions used unconventional chord progressions. He was considered the first major jazz player since Duke Ellington.

**Monkey Trial** See Scopes Trial.

**monograph** a scholarly treatise on a single topic, usually with extensive documentation.

**monokini** a single-piece or topless bathing suit.

**Monopoly** the trademarked name of a board game invented in 1933 and distributed by Parker Brothers, in which players buy fictional real estate.

**Monroe Doctrine** doctrine outlined by President James Monroe in 1823 barring European nations from subverting the independence movements in Latin America, or attempting to recolonize the continent. Directed principally against Spain, most of whose colonies had become independent early in the 1820s.

**Monroe, James** 1758–1831. Fifth president of the United States (1817–1825). He wrote the Monroe Doctrine and helped negotiate the Louisiana Purchase.

**Monroe, Marilyn** 1926–1962. Actress. Born Norma Jean Baker, Monroe starred in several movies in the 1950s and was the most famous sex symbol of her time. She died of a drug overdose at the age of 36, but remains a popular American icon.

**Montana** a state in the northwestern United States. Called the Treasure State, its capital is Helena and its largest city is Billings. The western meadowlark is the state bird and the bitterroot is the state flower. Abbreviated MT.

**Monticello** Thomas Jefferson's neoclassical home near Charlottesville, Virginia, built between 1768 and 1809.

**mood drug** a stimulant that has the ability to affect or alter one's state of mind.

**Moody, Dwight Lyman** 1837–1899. Evangelist. Moody was the creator of modern mass evangelism combining music and a message of salvation by grace.

**Moore, Marianne Craig**  1887–1972. Poet. Moore's meticulously crafted poems reflect a rare range and depth and a powerful vision of nature. Her *Selected Poems* appeared in 1935.

**Moral Majority**  a politically active conservative Christian group founded by Reverend JERRY FALWELL in the late 1970s to mobilize opposition to the prevailing liberal value systems and legislative programs.

**Mormons**  members of the Church of JESUS CHRIST OF LATTER-DAY SAINTS, founded by JOSEPH SMITH in 1830. Their religion, Mormonism, is based on *The Book of the Mormon*. Mormons originally practiced polygamy, but it has since been outlawed. They established the state of UTAH.

**morph**  to change the form, contours, and colors of an object in a television sequence by means of computer animation techniques.

**Moses, Grandma**  1860–1961. Painter. Born Anna Mary Robertson Moses, she was a primitive artist who painted rural scenes. She took up painting in her sixties and had her first exhibition when she was 80.

**Motherwell, Robert**  1915–1991. Painter. An abstract expressionist, Motherwell is best known for his series *Elegy to the Spanish Republic*.

**Motor City**  MOTOWN.

**Motor Town**  MOTOWN.

**Motown**  1. a nickname for Detroit, MICHIGAN, from *Motor Town*. The city is also known as *Motor City*. Detroit is the home of the American automobile industry. 2. a style of RHYTHM AND BLUES with a strong beat developed by Motown Records in Detroit, a pioneer in AFRICAN-AMERICAN music.

**Mount Marcy**  See ADIRONDACK MOUNTAINS.

**Mount McKinley**  a mountain in ALASKA, the highest in North America at 20,320 feet. Named after President WILLIAM MCKINLEY.

**Mount Rainier**  See CASCADE RANGE.

**Mount Rushmore**  a granite cliff in SOUTH DAKOTA where in the interwar years sculptor Gutzon Borglum carved 60-foot-high heads of four presidents: GEORGE WASHINGTON, THOMAS JEFFERSON, ABRAHAM LINCOLN, and THEODORE ROOSEVELT.

**Mount Saint Helens** a volcano in the CASCADE RANGE of WASHINGTON. Dormant from 1857, it erupted in 1980, spewing ashes for miles.

**Mount Vernon** the Georgian style home and riverfront plantation of GEORGE WASHINGTON in VIRGINIA. It is now a national shrine.

**mountain daylight time** the adjusted time in the Rocky Mountain region of the United States from early April to late October. It is six hours behind Greenwich time. Abbreviated MDT.

**mountain lion** a large wildcat of North and South America. Also called a *painter*, a *panther*, or a *puma*.

**mountain oysters** the testicles of a bull cooked and eaten as a food.

**mountain standard time** the time in the Rocky Mountain region of the United States from the last weekend in October to the first weekend in April. It is seven hours behind Greenwich time. Abbreviated MST.

*mountain lion*

**Mountain State** WEST VIRGINIA.

**movie ratings** a ratings system for movies devised by the Motion Picture Association of America in 1968. The rating codes themselves can change as the MPAA deems necessary. Some of the current movie ratings are: *G* for General Audiences (all ages admitted), *PG* for Parental Guidance Suggested (some material may not be suitable for children), *PG-13* for Parents Strongly Cautioned (some material may be inappropriate for children under 13), and *NC-17* for No Children Under 17 Admitted (age varies in some jurisdictions). A similar system was implemented for television shows. See TELEVISION RATINGS.

**MPAA** the Motion Picture Association of America, the organization that regulates the motion picture industry and assigns MOVIE RATINGS.

**M.S.** MASTER OF SCIENCE.

**MS** MISSISSIPPI. (The official two-letter post office abbreviation.)

**MSA** Metropolitan Statistical Area, a U.S. Bureau of Census geographical unit.

**MST** MOUNTAIN STANDARD TIME.

**MT** MONTANA. (The official two-letter post office abbreviation.)

**MTV** Music Television. A cable television network that broadcasts videos of songs and shows related to the ROCK AND ROLL music industry.

**muckraker** any crusading journalist who exposed corruption in government and private corporations at the turn of the century. Among the most prominent muckrakers were Lincoln Steffens (1836–1936; *The Shame of the Cities*, 1904), Ida Tarbell (1857–1944; *History of the Standard Oil Company*, 1904), and UPTON SINCLAIR (*The Jungle*, 1906).

**mugwump** a reform Republican who left the party during the 1884 election to vote for GROVER CLEVELAND. From the ALGONQUIN word for chief.

**Muir, John** 1838–1914. Naturalist. A major figure in the forest conservation movement, Muir was responsible for the establishment of YOSEMITE and Sequoia national parks.

**mule** a drug courier who conceals drugs in the intestines or other parts of his or her own body.

**multiculturalism** a social phenomenon in which diversity is accepted and encouraged, especially by allowing competing cultural traditions to flourish as distinctive and equal elements rather than being forced to assimilate into a dominant culture.

**multinational** a corporation with branches and plants or doing business in a number of countries. Also called transnational.

**Mumford, Lewis Charles** 1895–1990. Social historian and philosopher. Mumford became a pundit and a prophet of modern civilization, weighing in against the dehumanization of cities.

**muni** municipal bond.

**Murphy bed** a bed that folds into a closet or a space in a wall when not being used.

**Murphy's Law** any of a number of anecdotal principles that illustrate the absurdity of life and the constant intrusion of the irrational in everyday life. For example: If anything can go wrong, it will.

**Murrow, Edward R.** 1908–1965. News commentator. A commanding figure in the broadcast news industry from the 1930s to the 1960s, Murrow served as correspondent and producer for nearly 25 years.

**Museum of Modern Art** a museum of contemporary art in New York City. Abbreviated MOMA.

**mutual fund** a company that invests in stocks with the money received from its investors. Mutual funds are popular with small investors, because the fund decides what investments to make and the risk is low.

**muu-muu** a long, loose women's dress of Hawaiian origin.

**Muzak** a trademarked name for programmed soothing music played in offices, elevators, and stores. Also called ELEVATOR MUSIC.

**MVP** most valuable player. A sports designation awarded to the most valuable player of a game or a season.

**NAACP** National Association for the Advancement of Colored People. Usually pronounced *EN double A SEE PEE*. A national organization established in 1909 to integrate AFRICAN-AMERICANS fully by ending racial prejudice and intolerance and by providing equal opportunities in all aspects of life.

**Nabokov, Vladimir** 1899–1977. Writer. Russian-born Nabokov was an incomparable and elegant stylist who used wordplay and subtle allusions to create multiple layers of meaning. His most famous novel is *Lolita* (1955).

**Nader, Ralph** 1934–. Lawyer and consumer rights activist. Founder and tireless promoter of consumer rights, Nader has become synonymous with citizen action to combat business and government practices detrimental to public interest.

**Naderism** a social philosophy that opposes corporate practices detrimental to the best interests of consumers. From RALPH NADER, consumer rights activist.

**NAFTA** North American Free Trade Association, a trade-based economic union of Mexico, the United States, and Canada.

**nanotechnology** technology dealing with or creating submicroscopic objects.

**narc** a federal narcotics agent.

**narrowcasting** the transmission of television programming by cable.

**NASA** NATIONAL AERONAUTICS AND SPACE ADMINISTRATION.

**NASDAQ** NATIONAL ASSOCIATION OF SECURITIES DEALERS AUTOMATED QUOTATIONS.

**Nast, Thomas** 1840–1902. Cartoonist. Nast, the most important 19th-century political cartoonist, made history by exposing the TWEED RING and causing the downfall of TAMMANY HALL. He is also remembered for drawing the donkey and the elephant as symbols of the DEMOCRATIC PARTY and the REPUBLICAN PARTY, respectively, and for creating the roly-poly image of SANTA CLAUS.

**Nathan, George Jean** 1882–1958. Drama critic and writer. Nathan cofounded some of the most influential literary journals of the interwar years, including *The Smart Set*, *The American Mercury*, and *American Spectator*. In the 1920s Nathan was the most widely read and highest paid drama critic in the world.

**Nation, Carry** 1846–1911. Temperance leader. Nation's hatchet-bashing of saloons made temperance a national issue and helped to pass the Eighteenth Amendment, establishing PROHIBITION, in 1919.

**Nation of Islam** the official name for BLACK MUSLIMS.

**National Aeronautics and Space Administration** the government agency responsible for exploration of outer space, established in 1958. Abbreviated NASA.

**National Association for the Advancement of Colored People** NAACP.

**National Association of Securities Dealers Automated Quotations** the second largest stock market in the United States, established in 1971. Millions of securities for heavily traded over-the-counter stocks are exchanged each day. Abbreviated NASDAQ.

**National Basketball Association** the professional BASKETBALL league of the United States. Abbreviated NBA.

**National Collegiate Athletic Association** the governing organization of college and university athletic departments, founded in 1906. Abbreviated NCAA.

**National Educational Television** an agency that facilitates educational television programming in the United States. Abbreviated NET.

**National Endowment for the Humanities** an independent government agency that offers grants to people pursuing research and education in the humanities. Abbreviated NEH.

**National Football Conference** one of two divisions of the NATIONAL FOOTBALL LEAGUE. Abbreviated NFC.

**National Football League** the professional FOOTBALL league of the United States. Abbreviated NFL.

**National Hockey League** the professional hockey league of the United States. Abbreviated NHL.

**National Institutes of Health** the government agency within the DEPARTMENT OF HEALTH AND HUMAN SERVICES that conducts research for better health care and disease control. Abbreviated NIH.

**National League** one of the two professional baseball leagues in the United States. The other is the AMERICAN LEAGUE. Abbreviated NL.

**National Organization for Women** an organization that supports causes related to women. Founded in 1966, it promotes the passage of the EQUAL RIGHTS AMENDMENT. Abbreviated NOW.

**National Public Radio** a nonprofit, federally funded radio network. Abbreviated NPR.

**National Rifle Association** the primary organization for people who own and collect guns and other firearms. Abbreviated NRA.

**Native American** one of the indigenous people of the Americas, or one of their descendants, formerly known as an American INDIAN.

**Navajo** the second largest NATIVE AMERICAN tribe in the United States, found principally in the Southwest.

**NBA** NATIONAL BASKETBALL ASSOCIATION.

**NBC** the National Broadcasting Company, one of the three major television networks in the United States, along with ABC and CBS. NBC began daily television broadcasts in 1939. It owns and operates many stations across the country.

**NC** NORTH CAROLINA. (The official two-letter post office abbreviation.)

**NC-17** See MOVIE RATINGS.

**NCAA** NATIONAL COLLEGIATE ATHLETIC ASSOCIATION.

**ND** NORTH DAKOTA. (The official two-letter post office abbreviation.)

**NE** NEBRASKA. (The official two-letter post office abbreviation.)

**Nebraska** a state in the U.S. MIDWEST. Called the Cornhusker State, its capital is Lincoln and its largest city is Omaha. The goldenrod is Nebraska's state flower, and the western meadowlark is its state bird. Abbreviated NE.

**negative option** in merchandising, the obligation to return a card offering a product back to the sender within a specified time or to accept and pay for the product on its arrival.

**Negro** an AFRICAN-AMERICAN. Once widely used, the term is now considered inappropriate.

**NEH** NATIONAL ENDOWMENT FOR THE HUMANITIES.

**neoconservatism** a secular form of conservatism that favors some social reforms but is strongly opposed to big government and in favor of unregulated capitalism.

**NET** NATIONAL EDUCATIONAL TELEVISION.

**Nevada** a state in the western United States. Known as the Sagebrush State or the Silver State, its capital is Carson City and its largest city is LAS VEGAS. The mountain bluebird is Nevada's state bird, and the sagebrush is its state flower. Abbreviated NV.

**New Age** 1. a quasi-religious movement, drawn principally from Hindu, Buddhist, and American Indian religions, incorporating such concepts as holistic health, altered states of consciousness, and oneness with nature. 2. a form of music in which instrumental sounds are manipulated to create a quiescent and dreamy state of mind.

**New Deal** FRANKLIN DELANO ROOSEVELT's social and economic reform legislation, particularly the creation of a host of regulatory agencies and the institution of SOCIAL SECURITY.

**New England**  a section of the United States that includes the following eastern states: CONNECTICUT, MAINE, MASSACHUSETTS, NEW HAMPSHIRE, RHODE ISLAND, and VERMONT.

*New England Primer*  an early NEW ENGLAND grammar school textbook, first published around 1690 in Boston, MASSACHUSETTS, that included morally uplifting stories and prayers.

**New Frontier**  JOHN FITZGERALD KENNEDY's name for his legislative and political agenda designed to enhance America's technological and economic superiority.

**New Hampshire**  a state in the northeastern United States. Called the Granite State, its capital is Concord and its largest city is Manchester. Its state bird is the purple finch, and its state flower is the purple lilac. Abbreviated NH.

**New Jersey**  a state in the northeastern United States. Known as the Garden State, its capital is Trenton and its largest city is Newark. The eastern goldfinch is New Jersey's state bird, and the purple violet is its state flower. Abbreviated NJ.

**New Left**  student radicals of the 1960s who opposed the VIETNAM WAR and espoused a quasi-Marxist social revolution. Its founding document was the Port Huron Statement issued by The Students for a Democratic Society, the most Marxist of the New Left groups.

**New Mexico**  a state in the southwestern United States. Called the Land of Enchantment, its capital is Santa Fe and its largest city is Albuquerque. The yucca flower is New Mexico's state flower, and the roadrunner is its state bird. Abbreviated NM.

**New World**  North and South America; a term used by Europeans during the period of early colonization.

**New York**  a state in the northeastern United States. Known as the Empire State, its capital is Albany and its largest city is New York City. The state bird is the bluebird, and the state flower is the rose. Abbreviated NY.

**New York Stock Exchange**  the major American stock exchange headquartered in the financial district of MANHATTAN.

***New Yorker, The*** a literary magazine in New York City, founded by Harold Ross (1892–1951) in 1925, noted for its stylistic essays and cartoons.

**newbie** a newcomer to an INTERNET discussion group.

**newsgroup** an online discussion group organized by subject or topic.

**newsmaker** a newsworthy event or person.

***Newsweek*** a news magazine founded in 1933.

**NFC** NATIONAL FOOTBALL CONFERENCE.

**NFL** NATIONAL FOOTBALL LEAGUE.

**NH** NEW HAMPSHIRE. (The official two-letter post office abbreviation.)

**NHL** NATIONAL HOCKEY LEAGUE.

**Niagara Falls** a waterfall of the Niagara River between the Canadian Ontario Province and NEW YORK. An island separates the American side of the falls from the Canadian side, also known as Horseshoe Falls.

*Niagara Falls*

**nickelodeon** a penny arcade offering peep shows and gramaphone recordings in the 1880s and, later, silent films, all for a nickel.

**nicotine patch** a transdermal patch that emits nicotine that is then absorbed through the skin. Used to wean smokers from their habit.

**Niebuhr, Reinhold** 1892–1971. Protestant theologian. Niebuhr invented the nonorthodox Social Gospel, mixing politics, economics, and sociology. He influenced an entire generation of Protestant thinkers.

**Nielsen Rating**  the rating of the relative size of television audiences obtained by Nielsen Media Research through viewing diaries maintained by selected viewers and people meters.

**night riders**  the KU KLUX KLAN.

**NIH**  NATIONAL INSTITUTES OF HEALTH.

**NIMBY**  not in my back yard, opposition to the disposal of toxic or nuclear wastes within or close to residential communities.

**900 number**  a telephone number with an AREA CODE of 900. Such numbers are services that charge a fee, usually some amount of money per minute. Compare with 800 number. See also JUNK PHONE.

**Nisei**  a person born in America to Japanese parents. Many Nisei were forced into internment camps in 1942 after Japan bombed PEARL HARBOR in WORLD WAR II.

**Nixon, Richard Milhous**  1913–1994. Thirty-seventh president of the United States (1969–1974). Nixon was vice president under DWIGHT DAVID EISENHOWER. As president, he was commended for his groundbreaking visits to China and the Soviet Union. After WATERGATE, there was a movement to impeach Nixon, but he resigned, becoming the first president to do so.

**NJ**  NEW JERSEY. (The official two-letter post office abbreviation.)

**NL**  NATIONAL LEAGUE.

**NM**  NEW MEXICO. (The official two-letter post office abbreviation.)

**NOAA**  National Oceanic and Atmospheric Administration, a U.S. federal agency.

**no-load**  sales of stock to the public without sales commissions or investment management fees generally charged by brokers.

**North**  1. the northern states of the United States, usually those states north of the MASON-DIXON LINE; the UNION. Compare SOUTH. 2. a generic term for the industrialized and technologically advanced countries of North America and Europe as well as Japan, Australia, and New Zealand. Compare SOUTH. Also, FIRST WORLD.

**North Carolina** a state in the southeastern United States. Called the Tarheel State, its largest city is Charlotte and its capital is Raleigh. The cardinal is the state bird of North Carolina, and the dogwood is the state flower. Abbreviated NC.

**North Dakota** a state in the north-central United States, known as the Flickertail State. Its capital is Bismarck, and its largest city is Fargo. The western meadowlark is its state bird, and the wild prairie rose is its state flower. Abbreviated ND.

**North Star State** MINNESOTA.

***North Star, The*** See DOUGLASS, FREDERICK.

**NOW** NATIONAL ORGANIZATION FOR WOMEN.

**Now Generation** very fashionable people whose lifestyles conform to the latest trends.

**NPR** NATIONAL PUBLIC RADIO.

**NRA** NATIONAL RIFLE ASSOCIATION.

**numbered account** a bank account, especially in Switzerland, that is identified only by a secret number known only to the bank and the owner.

**numeraire** the currency unit used as the standard in international financial transactions and exchange rates. Since the end of WORLD WAR II, the numeraire has been the U.S. dollar.

**Nutmeg State** CONNECTICUT.

**NV** NEVADA. (The official two-letter post office abbreviation.)

**NY** NEW YORK. (The official two-letter post office abbreviation.)

**NYC** New York City, the largest city in the United States.

**NYNEX** New York New England Exchange. A regional Bell telephone company formed after the divestiture of AT&T in 1984, serving the states of MAINE, VERMONT, NEW HAMPSHIRE, MASSACHUSETTS, CONNECTICUT, RHODE ISLAND, and NEW YORK.

**NYSE** NEW YORK STOCK EXCHANGE.

# O

**O. Henry** 1862–1910. Short story writer. Born William Sydney Porter, he wrote short, simple stories that usually concluded with an ironic twist. One of his best-known stories is "The Gift of the Magi."

**Oakley, Annie** See WILD WEST SHOW.

**OASDI** old age, survivors, and disability insurance. Commonly known as SOCIAL SECURITY, a government program that provides benefits for the elderly and disabled. It is funded by a compulsory Social Security tax.

**Obie Awards** the annual awards for OFF-BROADWAY plays. Sponsored by *Village Voice*, a New York City newspaper.

**Occupational Safety and Health Administration** an agency established in 1970 under the jurisdiction of the Department of Labor to maintain safety and health standards in work environments, investigate violations of safety and health regulations, and to set penalties. Abbreviated OSHA.

**Ocean State** RHODE ISLAND.

**O'Connor, Flannery** 1925–1964. Novelist. O'Connor employed a typically Southern religious imagination to create grotesque and haunting stories. Her best-loved works include two novels, *Wise Blood* (1952) and *The Violent Bear It Away* (1960) and two collections of short stories, *A Good Man Is Hard to Find* (1955) and *Everything that Rises Must Converge* (published posthumously in 1965).

**Odets, Clifford** 1906–1963. Actor and playwright. Odets was a social activist who for 30 years used the theater to protest the ills of society.

**off-Broadway** unconventional and offbeat plays produced outside the main BROADWAY district in New York City and, by extension, mainline theater districts in other cities. Plays more experimental in scope are called OFF-OFF-BROADWAY.

**off-off-Broadway** theaters outside BROADWAY and OFF-BROADWAY and the low-budget and highly experimental plays they produce.

**OH** OHIO. (The official two-letter post office abbreviation.)

**O'Hara, John Henry** 1905–1970. Novelist. O'Hara faithfully portrayed the changing social mores in a number of popular novels, especially *Appointment in Samarra* (1934), *Ten North Frederick* (1955), and *From the Terrace* (1958).

**Ohio** a state in the U.S. MIDWEST. Called the Buckeye State, its largest city is Cleveland and its capital is Columbus. The scarlet carnation is the state flower, and the cardinal is the state bird. Abbreviated OH.

**O.K. Corral** a cattlepen in Tombstone, ARIZONA, scene of the most famous gunfight in the West in 1881 between WYATT EARP and his brothers and the CLANTON GANG.

**OK** 1. all right; satisfactory; expressing agreement or approval. Possibly from initials of "oll korrect," a humorous misspelling of "all correct," or from the O.K. Club, an organization of supporters of MARTIN VAN BUREN, whose nickname was *Old Kinderhook*. 2. OKLAHOMA. (The official two-letter post office abbreviation.)

**okay** See OK.

**O'Keeffe, Georgia** 1887–1986. Painter. Her paintings were vibrant with colors and celebrated the natural world with unique exuberance.

**Okies** a nickname for Oklahoman families who fled the state during the 1930s to escape drought and poverty.

**Oklahoma** a state in the southwestern United States. Known as the Sooner State, its capital and largest city is Oklahoma City. Its state flower is the mistletoe, and its state bird is the scissor-tailed flycatcher. Abbreviated OK.

**Old Blood and Guts** GEORGE S. PATTON.

**Old Blue Eyes** FRANK SINATRA.

**Old Colony State** MASSACHUSETTS.

**Old Dominion State** VIRGINIA.

**Old Faithful** a geyser in YELLOWSTONE NATIONAL PARK that shoots water 150 feet into the air approximately once an hour.

**Old Farmer's Almanac** the oldest almanac published in the United States, founded in 1793 by Robert Bailey Thomas.

**Old Fuss and Feathers** General Winfield Scott (1786–1866), WHIG PARTY presidential candidate.

**Old Glory** the flag of the United States of America. Also called STARS AND STRIPES.

**Old Hickory** ANDREW JACKSON.

**Old Kinderhook** MARTIN VAN BUREN.

*Old Glory/Stars and Stripes*

**Old Line State** MARYLAND.

**Old Man River** the MISSISSIPPI RIVER.

**Old Rough and Ready** ZACHARY TAYLOR.

**Old West** the western part of the United States in the late 19th century, characterized by lawlessness, battles with Native Americans, and a romanticized vision of the COWBOY's life. Also *Wild West*.

**Olmstead, Frederick Law** 1822–1903. Landscape architect. The first professional landscape architect, Olmstead was responsible for designing numerous public parks, including CENTRAL PARK in New

York City, and for promoting the National Parks movement with his advocacy of preservation.

**OMB** Office of Management and Budget, a U.S. government agency established in 1970 to replace the Bureau of the Budget.

**Onassis, Jackie** 1929–1994. Born Jacqueline Bouvier. The wife of JOHN FITZGERALD KENNEDY, she was FIRST LADY from 1961–1963, and later wife of Greek shipping tycoon, Aristotle Onassis (1906–1975). Also known as Jackie O.

**Oneida** an Indian nation of the IROQUOIS LEAGUE, and the only one to support the AMERICAN REVOLUTION.

**O'Neill, Eugene** 1888–1953. Playwright. Perhaps the most famous American playwright in the 20th century, he won the Nobel Prize for Literature in 1936. Of Irish extraction, O'Neill drew on his own turbulent life for his best plays, including *Anna Christie* (1921), *Mourning Becomes Electra* (1931), *The Iceman Cometh* (1946), and *Long Day's Journey into Night* (1956). His plays continue to be popular throughout the world.

**op-ed page** a newspaper page, generally opposite the editorial page, featuring unsolicited articles by well-known columnists and others.

**open enrollment** unrestricted admission to a state-run college or university to provide better opportunity for poorer students.

**opera window** a small ventless window on either side of the backseat of an automobile.

**OR** OREGON. (The official two-letter post office abbreviation.)

**oral history** history compiled through oral interviews with the participants or eyewitnesses of historical events and preserved as tapes and typed transcripts.

**Oregon** a state in the northwestern United States. Known as the Beaver State, its capital is Salem and its largest city is Portland. The oregon grape flower is its state flower, and the western meadowlark is its state bird. Abbreviated OR.

**Oregon Trail** trail from MISSOURI to OREGON, about 2,000 miles long, which was the principal covered-wagon trail for westward expansion from 1843 until the 1870s, when the railways made such trails obsolete.

**organized crime** criminal activities by members of a crime syndicate, such as the MAFIA.

**orphan drug** a drug that is needed by so few patients suffering from very rare diseases that it is not commercially profitable to manufacture.

**Oscar** See ACADEMY AWARDS.

**Osceola** c1803–1838. War leader of the Seminole Indians. Osceola resisted U.S. government orders to forcibly transfer Seminoles to OKLAHOMA.

**OSHA** OCCUPATIONAL SAFETY AND HEALTH ADMINISTRATION.

**Oswald, Lee Harvey** 1939–1963. Alleged assassin of JOHN FITZGERALD KENNEDY. He was arrested soon after Kennedy was killed in Dallas in 1963, and he was murdered by Jack Ruby, a nightclub owner, before he could come to trial. Oswald denied killing Kennedy.

**out** out of the closet; used of homosexuals who publicly announce their sexual orientation.

**outplacement** efforts to secure new employment for employees being discharged from a downsized corporation.

**outsert** a newspaper or magazine supplement distributed with the main paper wrapped in a separate bag.

**outsource** to assign to outside independent contractors work formerly done in-house.

**outtake** a shot or scene that is not used in the final edited version of a film.

**Oval Office** the executive office of the president of the United States in the WHITE HOUSE. Also used as a metaphor for presidential power.

**Ozarks** a mountain system stretching from northwestern ARKANSAS into MISSOURI, KANSAS, and OKLAHOMA, home of a backwoods culture and folklore.

# P

**PA** PENNSYLVANIA. (The official two-letter post office abbreviation.)

**pacific daylight time** the adjusted time in the westernmost contiguous United States from early April to late October. It is six hours behind Greenwich time. Abbreviated PDT.

**Pacific Rim** the countries that border the Pacific Ocean, especially Canada and the United States in North America, and Japan, China, the Philippines, Korea, and Indonesia in Asia.

**pacific standard time** the standard time in the western United States from late October to early April. It is seven hours behind Greenwich time. Abbreviated PST.

**Painted Desert** an area in northeastern ARIZONA known for its colorful sandstone formations.

**painter** variation of PANTHER.

**palimony** alimony paid to or claimed by a former POSSLQ.

**Palmetto State** SOUTH CAROLINA.

**pan** the horizontal movement of a movie camera from a fixed point.

**pancake** a thin round of batter cooked on a frying pan. Also called flapjack, hotcake, and griddle cake.

**Panhandle State** IDAHO.

**panther** a MOUNTAIN LION.

**paparazzo** a freelance photographer who pursues celebrities aggressively to take their pictures in possibly compromising or unflattering situations. (The plural is *paparazzi*.)

**paramedic** a person trained to give emergency medical care.

**paratransit** a system of transportation that supplements formal urban or mass-transit vehicles and uses automobiles, small buses, and vans without fixed schedules or routes.

**parish** 1. a political subdivision in LOUISIANA that is equivalent to the COUNTY in other states. 2. a district served by a local church, and the churchgoers of the district.

**park and ride** a facility for suburban commuters to use public transport for part of their commute by parking their cars at an intermediate station.

**Park Avenue** an exclusive shopping and residential area in New York City.

**Parker, Bonnie** See BONNIE AND CLYDE.

**Parker, Charlie "Bird"** 1920–1955. Jazz musician. Parker employed ingenious rhythm, pitch, and harmony to create authentic experiments in JAZZ sound. He is considered one of the greatest jazz saxophonists of all time.

**Parker, Dorothy** 1893–1967. Writer and critic. Many of Parker's satires appeared in *The New Yorker* magazine. Known for her biting wit, she was a prominent member of the ALGONQUIN ROUND TABLE.

**Parkman, Francis** 1823–1893. Historian. Parkman is best known for his magnum opus, *France and England in North America* (1892).

**parochial school** a private school supported by a church or a PARISH of a church.

**party call** See CONFERENCE CALL.

**passive restraint** a safety device, such as an air bag, that is automatically activated to protect a driver in the case of an accident.

**passive smoke** smoke from active smokers that is inhaled by nonsmokers in the same room or vicinity. Also called *secondhand smoke*.

**pathography** a biography that focuses on exposing the scandals and failures of its subject, rather than being an objective and balanced study.

**patronage system** a system that allows a government official to use his power to appoint his chosen people to office or to use favors to gain constituents.

**Patton, George S.** 1885–1945. U.S. general. Patton, a brilliant tank commander, led the Allied forces during WORLD WAR II. He was nicknamed OLD BLOOD AND GUTS.

**Pauling, Linus** 1901–1994. Scientist and peace activist. Pauling won two Nobel Prizes, the first in 1954 in chemistry for his work on chemical bonds and molecular structure, and the second for peace in 1962.

*George S. Patton*

**PBS** PUBLIC BROADCASTING SYSTEM.

**PDT** PACIFIC DAYLIGHT TIME.

**Peace Corps** a service corps founded during the Kennedy Administration to send volunteers and young skilled workers to underdeveloped countries to participate in developmental work.

**peace dividend** savings from the reduced defense budget transferred to social programs in the wake of the end of the COLD WAR.

**peace pipe** a tobacco pipe with a reed stem used by NATIVE AMERICANS on ceremonial occasions.

**peace sign** a V-shaped sign made with the fingers as a symbol of peace and friendship.

**Peach State** GEORGIA.

**peanut butter** ground, roasted peanuts, sometimes with added sugar and/or salt. A popular sandwich ingredient, especially with jelly.

**Pearl Harbor** a U.S. naval base on the island of Oahu, HAWAII, site of the surprise aerial attack by Japanese bombers on December 7, 1941, described by FRANKLIN DELANO ROOSEVELT as a "date which will live in infamy." The incident triggered a U.S. declaration of war against Japan.

**Peculiar Institution** a euphemistic term used to describe slavery in the 18th and 19th centuries.

**Peculiar People** See QUAKERS.

**Pei, Ieoh Ming** 1917–. Architect. Immigrating to the United States in 1935, Pei became one of the foremost practitioners of Late Modernism with stirring examples of government and academic buildings and museums. Among his creations are the Denver Mile High Center (1956), Boston's John Hancock Tower (1976), and the John F. Kennedy Library in Boston (1979).

**Pelican State** LOUISIANA.

**Penn, William** 1644–1718. Colonial leader and Quaker. Penn founded the colony of PENNSYLVANIA in 1681 on land granted him by royal charter.

**pennant** the annual championship of each of the two major BASEBALL leagues.

**Pennsylvania** a state in the northeastern United States. Known as the Keystone State, its capital is Harrisburg and its largest city is Philadelphia. The state flower is the mountain laurel, and the state bird is the ruffed grouse. Abbreviated PA.

**Pennsylvania Dutch** descendants of the German immigrants who settled in eastern PENNSYLVANIA in the 17th and 18th centuries.

Dutch is a folk corruption of Deutsch, or German. A small group within this community is known as the AMISH.

**Pentagon** a building in the shape of a pentagon in Arlington, VIRGINIA, that houses the DEPARTMENT OF DEFENSE and its various agencies. Also used as a collective term for the military.

**peoplemeter** a remote controlled device recording the television-viewing habits of people by means of buttons punched when a particular show is watched.

**Peoria** a quintessential small town in ILLINOIS, noted for its small town attitudes and social mores.

**Pepsi** the trademarked name of a popular soft drink invented by NORTH CAROLINA pharmacist Caleb Bradham in 1898. Its chief rival is COCA-COLA.

**Persian Gulf War** 1991 military struggle that began as a response to Iraq's invasion of Kuwait and its disregard of UN resolutions. Also called Operation Desert Storm, the conflict lasted six weeks, ending upon Iraq's acceptance of UN resolutions. The superior forces and equipment of the United States greatly overpowered Iraq.

**Petrified Forest National Park** a national park in eastern ARIZONA that contains many petrified trees. It is part of the PAINTED DESERT.

**peyote** a cactus found in the southwestern United States whose top contains a drug that produces hallucinations.

**PG** See MOVIE RATINGS.

**PG-13** See MOVIE RATINGS.

**PGA** Professional Golfers' Association. The men's league of professional golfers.

**Ph.D.** *Philosophiae Doctor.* Latin: Doctor of Philosophy. The highest graduate degree awarded for research in a particular study.

**phi beta kappa** an honorary fraternity established in 1776.

**phone-in** See CALL-IN.

**photo-op** a photo-opportunity, an occasion for a publicity-hungry person to gain media attention.

**PHS** PUBLIC HEALTH SERVICE.

**Phyfe, Duncan** 1768–1854. Furniture maker. The greatest of all American furniture makers, Phyfe was the creator and leading exponent of the American Federal and American Empire styles of furniture making.

**Pierce, Franklin** 1804–1869. Fourteenth president of the United States (1853–1857).

**Pikes Peak** a tall mountain in the ROCKY MOUNTAINS in COLORADO. Its location on the edge of the GREAT PLAINS makes it conspicuous. It was named for its discoverer, explorer Zebulon Pike (1779–1813).

**Pilgrims** a popular name for the early colonists who sailed on the MAYFLOWER and founded PLYMOUTH COLONY in MASSACHUSETTS in 1620 under the leadership of the Pilgrim Fathers, such as WILLIAM BREWSTER and WILLIAM BRADFORD. They called themselves saints. Also known as PURITANS.

**Pine Tree State** MAINE.

**pink** the color associated with Communist or leftist sympathizers.

**pink-collar** of an occupation or profession in which women predominate or for which women are said to have special innate skills.

**Pinkertons** the Pinkerton Agency, the first detective firm in the United States, founded by detective Alan Pinkerton (1819–1894). The firm was active in the suppression of labor unrest and in guarding the WELLS FARGO and other stagecoach companies in the 19th century.

**pinstriper** a business executive, from the pinstripe suits commonly worn by them.

**places** the call given by a stage manager before the curtain rises and a play begins.

**Plain People** See AMISH.

**plantation** 1. in Colonial times, a synonym for a colony in NEW ENGLAND. 2. in the SOUTH, a large estate with a mansion that had quarters for slaves.

**Plath, Sylvia** 1932–1963. Poet. Plath's emotional turmoil was reflected in poems etched in grotesque humor and savage irony. Her works include *The Bell Jar* (1963).

**plea bargain** in a criminal case, an agreement between the prosecution and the defense by which the latter pleads guilty to a lesser charge so as to avoid a long and costly trial for a more serious offense.

**Pledge of Allegiance** a public declaration of loyalty to the American flag and the United States, reportedly written by Francis Bellamy for the Columbus Quadricentennial in 1892. It is routinely recited in some schools and at meetings.

**plum book** an informal publication used by an incoming president that lists all government positions that are due to be filled in a new administration.

**plumber** a person specially assigned to investigate and stop leaks of confidential official information.

**Plumed Knight** nickname of James G. Blaine (1830–1893), Republican presidential candidate in 1884.

**pluralism** tolerance for and acceptance of a society or group consisting of many diverse cultures. See also MULTICULTURALISM.

**Plymouth Colony** a colony in present-day MASSACHUSETTS settled by MAYFLOWER passengers in 1620. In 1691 it was absorbed into the Massachusetts Bay Colony.

**Plymouth Compact** a document or covenant signed by 41 male passengers on the MAYFLOWER jointly committing themselves to "due submission and obedience to a civil body politick."

**Plymouth Rock** a beach boulder at Plymouth, MASSACHUSETTS, marking the original landing site of the PILGRIMS as they stepped out of the MAYFLOWER and into the NEW WORLD.

**Pocahontas** c1595–1617. Indian princess, daughter of Powhatan, head of VIRGINIA's Powhatan Confederacy. According to legend, she saved Captain JOHN SMITH's life at the JAMESTOWN colony. She eventually was baptized as Lady Rebecca and then married colonist John Rolfe and traveled with him to London.

**podunk** a dull small town.

**Poe, Edgar Allan** 1809–1849. Writer, poet. One of the giants of American literature, Poe created a unique genre that combined horror with pathos and influenced many generations of writers. Among his famous poems is *The Raven* (1845), and among his stories, "The Pit and the Pendulum" (1842). His "Murders in the Rue Morgue" (1841) was a pioneering detective story.

**policy wonk** a serious student of public policy issues who spends considerable time on their analysis.

*Edgar Allan Poe*

**Polk, James Knox** 1795–1849. Eleventh president of the United States (1845–1849).

**Pollock, Jackson** 1912–1956. Painter. Considered one of the most revolutionary among Modernists, Pollock pioneered a method of painting in which he poured paint onto canvases.

**Pontiac** c1720–1769. Ottawa Indian chief. He led an organized rebellion against the British that ended in 1765.

**Pony Express** the horseback mail delivery system, begun in 1860 and discontinued in 1861, which linked MISSOURI to CALIFORNIA through a series of relay stations. It made an average trip between the two states in about 10 days, but it was vulnerable to attacks from INDIANS and highwaymen.

**poorboy** a type of SUB(MARINE SANDWICH) popular in New Orleans, LOUISIANA, often containing seafood.

**pop art** an unconventional art form of the 1950s and 1960s, associated with ANDY WARHOL, ROY LICHTENSTEIN, and others, that incorporates images from popular culture. It produced garish and vulgar images of everyday objects.

**popcorn** corn kernels which have been heated to the point of bursting. A popular snack food, especially at movie theaters, it is usually coated with butter and salt.

**Populist** any of several agrarian reformers who mounted serious third-party campaigns for the presidency at the turn of the century.

**Porter, Cole** 1893–1964. Songwriter. Porter wrote lyrics for more than 20 successful BROADWAY musicals.

**Porter, Katherine Anne** 1890–1980. Short story writer. Her well-crafted short stories depict a world of people in the shadow of misfortunes and calamities that defy understanding. Her only novel, *Ship of Fools* (1962), was made into a movie.

**POSSLQ** person of the opposite sex sharing living quarters, a census term for unmarried persons living together as a couple.

**Post, Emily** 1872–1960. Authority on etiquette. Post wrote *Etiquette: The Blue Book of Social Usage* (1922), which quickly became the authority on social behavior and manners in America.

**pot roast** a piece of meat cooked in a pot with liquid.

**potato chip** a very thin slice of potato, fried until crisp and salted, which is eaten as a snack food.

**potlatch** a ceremony of the NATIVE AMERICANS in the Pacific Northwest in which expensive gifts were given or burned as a symbol of the giver's public disposal of wealth.

**potluck** 1. a meal that consists of whatever food is on hand; a meal for which there is no special preparation or planning. 2. a dinner where each diner brings some kind of food to be served to everyone else.

**potpie** a pie with a filling that is savory, not sweet.

**POTUS** code name of the president of the United States.

**Pound, Ezra Loomis** 1885–1972. Poet. Considered the poet's poet, Pound was a mentor to some of the greatest modern poets, and he

173

established the poetic conventions that still dominate the poet's craft. Master of spare language, rich allusive narration, and vivid imagery, Pound's later years were spent as a mental patient in a hospital, incarcerated for collaboration with the Nazis in WORLD WAR II.

**POW** prisoner of war. A member of the military held captive by the enemy.

**powder room** RESTROOM.

**Powell, John Wesley** 1834–1902. Explorer of the Green and Colorado rivers. Powell was head of the U.S. Geological Survey and chief of the Bureau of Ethnology at the SMITHSONIAN INSTITUTION.

**power broker** a person who uses his or her influence to help others achieve or use power, generally with ulterior motives.

**PR** PUERTO RICO. (The official two-letter post office abbreviation.)

**prairie** the GREAT PLAINS, stretching from the MISSISSIPPI RIVER to the ROCKY MOUNTAINS.

**prairie schooner** a COVERED WAGON.

**Prairie State** ILLINOIS.

**prayer breakfast** a morning get-together of Christian laypersons and pastors that combines breakfast and intercessionary prayer.

**Presley, Elvis** 1935–1977. ROCK AND ROLL artist. Presley was a superstar who reigned as the king of rock music from 1955 to his death in 1977. His early hits included "Hound Dog" and "Blue Suede Shoes." His early death (reportedly caused by drug overuse) only enhanced his image as a tragic icon of American culture. Popularly known as The King, his estate, GRACELAND, is a popular tourist attraction.

**primary care** health care confined to basic diagnosis and treatment of simple illnesses or problems, as distinguished from specialized care of acute illnesses.

**prime time** of television programs shown between 7 and 11 p.m., the time when the largest potential audience can be reached.

**Princeton University** one of the big three among the IVY LEAGUE schools, founded in 1746 as The College of New Jersey for the purpose of training clergymen. Its college building, Nassau Hall, was the nation's capitol during the REVOLUTIONARY WAR.

**prisoner of conscience** political prisoner.

**proactive** anticipating trends and actively involved in devising solutions, as opposed to being reactive or merely responding to problems.

**pro-choice** supporting the unfettered rights of a woman to have an abortion and a broad range of other rights for women.

**product liability** the legal responsibility of a manufacturer for punitive damages for illness or injury caused by its products.

**progressive rock** an experimental form of ROCK AND ROLL music, also known as heavy rock.

**progressive tax** a tax that is graduated according to the ability to pay and whose incidence rises proportionally at higher levels of income.

**Prohibition** the period from 1919 to 1933, during which the manufacture, sale, and import of alcoholic beverages were outlawed in the United States by the Eighteenth Amendment to the CONSTITUTION. It resulted in the growth of organized crime, which controlled the illegal manufacture and sale of liquor. The Twenty-first Amendment later repealed the Eighteenth Amendment, ending Prohibition. See also VOLSTEAD ACT, TEMPERANCE MOVEMENT.

**pro-life** supporting the rights of fetuses and opposing women's rights to abortion on demand.

**Protestant ethic** an ethic derived from Calvinism that places a high value on thrift and dedication to work rather than on immediate gratification of desires.

**PST** PACIFIC STANDARD TIME.

**psychobabble** jargon used by psychiatrists or counselors to explain complex mental phenomena in hard-to-understand terms.

**PTA** parent-teacher association. An organization of parents and teachers within a school district who meet to address issues facing the school.

**Public Broadcasting System** a television network whose operating income comes from federal funds and private donations instead of the revenue from commercials. Abbreviated PBS, the network broadcasts many educational and cultural programs.

**public enemy** any notorious criminal on the FBI's most-wanted list.

**Public Health Service** an administration within the DEPARTMENT OF HEALTH AND HUMAN SERVICES that regulates and coordinates federal health policies. Abbreviated PHS.

**Pueblo** 1. NATIVE AMERICAN people of the Southwest, including the Hopi and the ZUNI, who live in villages of ADOBES. 2. the settlements of these people, usually consisting of clusters of ADOBE buildings.

**Puerto Rico, Commonwealth of** a possession of the United States located in the Caribbean Sea. San Juan is its capital and largest city. Abbreviated PR.

**puka** a small, perforated white beach shell of HAWAII that is strung on a wire to form a necklace or bracelet.

**Pulitzer, Joseph** 1847–1911. Newspaper publisher. Pulitzer was a Hungarian immigrant who built up a newspaper empire based on his 1878 acquisition of the *St. Louis Dispatch* and *Evening Post*, which he merged into the *Post-Dispatch*. In 1883 he acquired the *New York World* and molded it into a major newspaper. The PULITZER PRIZE is named after him.

**Pulitzer Prize** any one of several annual awards in journalism, literature, and music established by publisher JOSEPH PULITZER. The Pulitzer Prize was first awarded in 1917 and is administered by COLUMBIA UNIVERSITY.

**pull date** the date stamped on packaged foods after which they should be pulled off the shelves.

**Pullman car** a railroad sleeping car produced by the Pullman Palace Car Company, founded in 1867 by George Mortimer Pullman (1831–1897).

**pulp magazine**  a cheap fiction magazine printed on pulpwood paper. Like DIME NOVELS before them, pulp magazines provided an entire generation of readers in the late 19th century with soft reading.

**puma**  a MOUNTAIN LION.

**punk**  a loud and aggressive form of ROCK AND ROLL music that reflects emotional despair as well as political anger.

**Puritans**  English religious dissenters, among whom were the PILGRIMS who came to America aboard the MAYFLOWER. Their theology and social institutions dominated NEW ENGLAND during the formative years of the American colonies.

**Purple Heart**  a decoration given to members of the armed forces for extraordinary bravery.

**Quakers** English religious dissenters, properly called the Religious Society of Friends, so called because of their quaking movements during service. Also called Peculiar People because of their pacifism, plain dress, and distinctive speech. They were particularly strong in PENNSYLVANIA, which had been established by WILLIAM PENN as a haven and as a Holy Experiment in Quaker living.

**quality-of-life offenses** offenses that diminish the ability of citizens to live a healthful and positive life, particularly prostitution, noise pollution, gambling, and drug trafficking.

**quality of life** the sum total of the tangible and intangible factors that contribute to a positive, healthful, and satisfying life.

**quarterback** a key position in FOOTBALL. The quarterback decides strategy, gives the signals at the beginning of each play, and carries or passes the football.

**Queen of Soul** ARETHA FRANKLIN.

**quilt** a heavy bedcovering made from different pieces of material stitched together, commonly made at quilting parties.

**Quonset hut** a semicylindrical metal building, generally prefabricated, first used during WORLD WAR II. From Quonset Point, RHODE ISLAND, where it was first built.

*a bed covered with a quilt*

# R

**R & B** RHYTHM AND BLUES, BLUES music with a strong rhythmic beat.

**rabbit ears** a portable television antenna with two adjustable diagonal rods.

**radical chic** extreme liberal ideology flaunted by the fashionable people in society to enhance their progressive image.

**Radio City Music Hall** the largest indoor theater in the world, built in 1932 in Rockefeller Center in New York City and noted for its 10,000-square-foot stage and Art Deco foyer.

**ragtime** a predecessor of JAZZ, marked by lilting melodies and elaborately syncopated rhythm and usually played on the piano. First popular between 1890 and 1920, its popularity surged again in the 1970s. SCOTT JOPLIN was its pioneer.

**rain date** an alternative date for an outdoor performance or activity canceled because of bad weather.

**rainbow coalition** a multiracial alliance of political activists, especially during an election.

**rainmaker** an aggressive salesperson or executive with many influential contacts who brings in considerable new business.

**rap music** AFRICAN-AMERICAN musical form in which rhythmic free-form poetry, usually with an urban theme, is spoken with a minimum of orchestration. From *rap*, African-American slang for talk.

**rap sheet**  a police blotter or record.

**rapper**  a musician who performs RAP MUSIC, a form of AFRICAN-AMERICAN music in which words are not sung but recited against a rhythmic background.

**rapture**  in Christian eschatology, the transport of all believers to heaven at the time of Christ's Second Coming.

**rat race**  a ruthless struggle to survive and make a living, especially in a profession without any redeeming features.

**RD**  rural delivery. Postal delivery to rural, outlying areas. Compare to RFD.

**readeo**  a book and its companion videocassette packaged and sold together.

***Reader's Digest***  a popular monthly founded in 1922 by DeWitt and Lila Acheson Wallace. Until the late 1980s it was the largest-selling magazine in the world.

**Reagan, Ronald**  1911–. Fortieth president of the United States (1981–1989). Reagan was a HOLLYWOOD actor and the governor of CALIFORNIA before being elected president. See REAGANOMICS.

**Reaganomics**  conservative economic policies introduced by President RONALD REAGAN's administration in the 1980s involving tax cuts and domestic spending cuts.

**real McCoy, the**  the original and genuine stuff or person. Possibly from its use to distinguish boxer "Kid" McCoy (1873–1940) from his numerous imitators.

**reality check**  an assessment of whether one's ideas and plans correspond to real-life situations or can withstand real-life pressures.

**Reconstruction**  the period after the CIVIL WAR in which the former CONFEDERATE states were once again made part of the United States. The states that had seceded were required to set up new governments, often with CARPETBAGGERS, and pass the Thirteenth and Fourteenth amendments (which outlawed slavery and denied former Confederates any public office) before gaining readmittance.

Areas of the SOUTH that were devastated by the war were rebuilt during this period.

**red** color associated with the Communist Party. Hence, as a derogative, Communist.

**redlining** a form of discrimination practiced by bankers and mortgage lenders against blighted inner cities inhabited mostly by AFRICAN-AMERICANS and poor people.

**redneck** a derogatory term for a poor white person from the rural SOUTH.

**redwood** a species of SEQUOIA. Its wood is very resistant to decay.

**reggae** AFRICAN-AMERICAN music of Jamaican origin combining elements of SOUL MUSIC, CALYPSO, and ROCK AND ROLL, featuring a strongly accentuated offbeat.

*redwood*

**registered nurse** someone who has a degree in nursing, has passed a state board examination, and is licensed to practice nursing. Abbreviated RN.

**relationship marketing** marketing strategies targeted less at selling products than at creating and maintaining the loyalty of customers to a brand or service.

**Remington, Frederic** 1861–1909. Artist of the OLD WEST. Remington's oils and sculptures of COWBOYS, cavalrymen, and NATIVE AMERICANS established a new genre.

**Renwick, James** 1818–1895. Architect. Renwick spearheaded the Gothic Revival with his St. Patrick's Cathedral in New York City and the original SMITHSONIAN INSTITUTION building.

**representative** a member of the HOUSE OF REPRESENTATIVES. Representatives are elected by voters in the district of the state they represent and serve two-year terms. They must meet age, residency, and citizenship requirements.

**Republican Party**  a conservative, probusiness political party founded in 1854 for opposing slavery in the Sᴏᴜᴛʜ.

**residual**  a royalty or fee received by a performing artist every time a commercial or television show in which he or she participated is replayed.

**restroom**  euphemism for a public toilet. Also called a *powder room*, especially by women.

**retirement community**  a residential community of mainly elderly people.

**Reuben sandwich**  a sandwich consisting of corned beef, Swiss cheese, and sauerkraut.

**Reuther, Walter Philip**  1907–1970. Labor leader. As president of the United Automobile Workers of America (UAW), Reuther made it a force in national politics.

**Revere, Paul**  1735–1818. Rᴇᴠᴏʟᴜᴛɪᴏɴᴀʀʏ Wᴀʀ hero. Revere is best known for alerting colonists in Mᴀꜱꜱᴀᴄʜᴜꜱᴇᴛᴛꜱ during the night about oncoming British troops. The story of his nighttime warning was popularized by Hᴇɴʀʏ Wᴀᴅꜱᴡᴏʀᴛʜ Lᴏɴɢꜰᴇʟʟᴏᴡ in *Paul Revere's Ride*.

**reverse discrimination**  discrimination against whites or members of other culturally dominant groups either by Aꜰʀɪᴄᴀɴ-Aᴍᴇʀɪᴄᴀɴꜱ or by government agencies or educational institutions following ᴀꜰꜰɪʀᴍᴀᴛɪᴠᴇ ᴀᴄᴛɪᴏɴ guidelines.

**Revised Standard Version**  an American Protestant version of the Bible, translated from the original Greek and published in 1952.

**Revolutionary War**  also called the *American Revolution*. The war (1775–1783) fought by the ᴛʜɪʀᴛᴇᴇɴ ᴄᴏʟᴏɴɪᴇꜱ for independence from Great Britain. The colonists, unhappy with British rule, were led by Gᴇᴏʀɢᴇ Wᴀꜱʜɪɴɢᴛᴏɴ and aided by the French. The Treaty of Paris (1783) officially ended the war.

**RFD**  rural free delivery, an older term for rural delivery service.

**Rhode Island** a state in the northeastern United States. Called the Ocean State, its capital and largest city is Providence. Its state bird is the Rhode Island redbird, and its state flower is the violet. Rhode Island is the smallest state in the United States. Abbreviated RI.

**Rhodes scholarship** any scholarship for study at Oxford University, England, established under the will of Cecil Rhodes, a British-born South African statesman and philanthropist.

**rhythm and blues** AFRICAN-AMERICAN music characterized by rich sounds created by electric guitars and saxophones. Abbreviated R & B.

**RI** RHODE ISLAND. (The official two-letter post office abbreviation.)

**RICO Act** Racketeer Influenced and Corrupt Organizations Act. A federal statute providing legislation to curb the influence of organized crime.

**Riley, James Whitcomb** 1849–1916. Poet. Riley is best known for his homey verses, including *Little Orphan Annie.*

**Rip Van Winkle** a character in WASHINGTON IRVING's story of the same name, who sleeps through a 20-year period and wakes up to find a startlingly changed world. Often used as a metaphor.

**RN** REGISTERED NURSE.

**roadkill** the carcass of an animal that has been hit and killed by a vehicle on a highway.

**Roanoke Colony** the first English colony in the NEW WORLD, established on an island off the coast of NORTH CAROLINA in the 1580s by Sir Walter Raleigh. It vanished without a trace within about five years and is known as the *Lost Colony.*

**Roaring Twenties** the 1920s, the decade when PROHIBITION spawned gang violence, bootlegging, and sexual license.

**robber baron** any of a number of captains of industry in the late 19th and early 20th centuries who gained enormous wealth through unethical or illegal means.

183

**Robbins, Jerome** 1918–. Choreographer, dancer. Robbins combined classical dance idioms and the American vernacular dance styles to create new and popular dance ensembles.

**Robeson, Paul** 1898–1976. AFRICAN-AMERICAN entertainer. Robeson excelled as an actor, athlete, and singer, but was hounded during the MCCARTHY ERA for his alleged Communist sympathies.

**rock** ROCK AND ROLL.

**rock and roll** (also *rock 'n' roll, rock.*) a musical idiom combining RHYTHM AND BLUES, JAZZ, and COUNTRY MUSIC, originally associated with ELVIS PRESLEY, CHUCK BERRY, and Bill Haley. It has a strong beat and a simple repetitious melody played with a two-beat rhythm that accents every second beat with instruments. Later rock and roll incorporated a variety of other styles and generated spinoff styles such as GLITTER ROCK, PUNK, and ACID ROCK.

**rock 'n' roll** ROCK AND ROLL.

**Rock, the** ALCATRAZ.

**Rockwell, Norman** 1894–1978. Illustrator. The most influential illustrator of his time, Rockwell portrayed an ideal America, translating his visions of a simple life into almost photographic illustrations for a number of magazines, particularly the *Saturday Evening Post*.

**Rocky Mountains** a large mountain range in western North America. It extends about 2,000 miles, from ALASKA to Mexico.

**rodeo** a form of entertainment of Mexican origin in which COWBOYS exhibit their skills in bronco busting, bull riding, calf roping, and steer wrestling.

**Rodgers, Richard** 1902–1979. Composer. Partner of Lorenz Hart and OSCAR HAMMERSTEIN II, Rodgers helped to create nearly 40 BROADWAY shows and shaped the course of American musical drama. His most enduring successes were *The King and I* (1951) and *The Sound of Music* (1959).

***Roe v. Wade*** a 1973 Supreme Court decision legalizing abortion and establishing a woman's right to privacy as a constitutional right.

**Roethke, Theodore** 1908–1963. Poet. Roethke's fascination with the mysteries of the human psyche produced powerful poetic images. Among his best-known works is *Words for the Wind* (1958).

**role model** a person who exhibits the ideal qualities and traits that could be emulated by his or her peers.

***Rolling Stone*** an iconoclastic magazine founded in New York City in 1967, considered by some to be the voice of the counterculture. The name was drawn from the rock band, the Rolling Stones.

**Roosevelt, Franklin Delano** 1882–1945. Thirty-second president of the United States (1933–1945). He instituted NEW DEAL reforms and led the country during World War II. He was elected for an unprecedented four terms. Also see BRAIN TRUST, FIRESIDE CHATS.

**Roosevelt, Theodore** 1858–1919. Twenty-sixth president of the United States (1901–1909). Roosevelt served in the SPANISH-AMERICAN WAR as a member of the ROUGH RIDERS and won the Nobel Peace Prize in 1906. His likeness is carved into MOUNT RUSHMORE.

*Franklin Delano Roosevelt*

**root beer** a soft drink based on an herbal tea recipe, developed by Philadelphia druggist Charles Hires.

**root beer float** a glass or mug of ROOT BEER with one or more scoops of ice cream floating on top.

**Rose Bowl** a college FOOTBALL game played each year on January 1, after the regular season, in Pasadena, CALIFORNIA. The Tournament of Roses Parade, a parade of floats decorated with roses and other flowers, always precedes the game.

**Ross, Betsy** 1752–1836. Seamstress. Though now widely disputed, it was once thought that Ross sewed the first American flag.

**Rotary club** a club belonging to Rotary International, a public service organization of professional businesspeople formed in 1905. Rotary clubs focus on community activities and humanitarian projects.

**ROTC** Reserve Officers' Training Corps, a U.S. Army program on college campuses for recruiting army officers.

**Roth, Philip** 1933–. Novelist. Roth used satire to explore Jewish culture enveloped by middle-American value systems. Among his acclaimed works are *Goodbye, Columbus* (1959), a collection of short stories, and the novel *Portnoy's Complaint* (1969).

**Rothko, Mark** 1903–1970. Painter. Rothko's paintings are notable for their simplicity of form and color without the burden of imagery or allusions.

**Rough Riders** in the SPANISH-AMERICAN WAR, the First Regiment of the U.S. Cavalry Volunteers, in which THEODORE ROOSEVELT was a colonel. Their charge on San Juan Hill brought them fame.

**Rubinstein, Arthur** 1887–1982. Pianist. A masterly performer on the piano, Rubinstein was a child prodigy who fulfilled the promise of his early years all the way up until his death.

**Ruby, Jack** See OSWALD, LEE HARVEY.

**rummage sale** a sale, usually held by a church or a charity to raise money, of miscellaneous items that have been donated.

**rush** the print of the camera footage from a single day's shooting. Also called *daily*.

**Rush, Benjamin** 1745–1813. Physician. One of the leading physicians of the REVOLUTIONARY WAR era, Rush was a fervent champion of a number of reforms that were far ahead of the times, including temperance, opposition to tobacco, public education, and prison reform.

**Rust Belt** the northeastern and midwestern states where heavy industry, such as steel, is concentrated.

**rustler** a person who steals cattle, usually a bandit in the OLD WEST.

**Ruth, Babe** 1895–1948. Baseball player. Ruth, who played for the Boston Red Sox and the New York Yankees, is a baseball legend. Nicknamed the *Sultan of Swat*, his greatest accomplishment was hitting 60 home runs in one season (1927).

**RV** recreational vehicle.

# S

**Sacagawea** c1786–1812. Shoshone woman and wife of a French trapper. She guided the LEWIS AND CLARK EXPEDITION through the ROCKY MOUNTAINS.

**SADD** Students Against Drunk Driving. A student organization whose goal is to reduce alcohol-related driving accidents and deaths.

**safe sex** sexual intercourse in which the couple adopts precautions to avoid conception or the transmission of sexual diseases.

**sagebrush** a small shrub with flowers, native to the western United States.

**Sagebrush State** NEVADA.

**saguaro cactus** a tall (20- to 40-foot), slow-growing, branching cactus that grows in the SONORAN DESERT of ARIZONA and Northern Mexico.

*saguaro cactus*

**Saint-Gaudens, Augustus** 1848–1907. Sculptor. The dominant American sculptor of the 19th century, Saint-Gaudens's works adorn some of the most important public monuments. He was also widely known for his portrait reliefs, which comprise almost two-thirds of his works.

**salad bar** an assortment of vegetables, dressings, and other salad ingredients presented in separate compartments in a bar-shaped stand for individuals who want to create their own salads. Salad bars are found in some restaurants and supermarkets.

**Salem witch trials** trials for witchcraft, a crime in the early Colonial era, which took place in the town of Salem, MASSACHUSETTS in 1692. As a result of the trials, 19 women were hanged.

**salsa** Hispanic dance music mixing Afro-Caribbean rhythms, Cuban big-band dance melodies, JAZZ, and ROCK AND ROLL.

**SALT** Strategic Arms Limitation Talks, multilateral negotiations on arms control and disarmament.

**saltwater taffy** TAFFY made with salted water.

**Salvation Army** a Christian social outreach mission founded by English evangelist William Booth (1829–1912). It expanded into the United States in 1880 and since then has become known for its work among the destitute and the underprivileged.

**San Andreas Fault** zone of faults or hidden fissures in the tectonic plates, extending along the coast of northern CALIFORNIA, toward the head of the Gulf of California, making the region highly vulnerable to earthquakes.

**San Juan Capistrano** a Spanish mission in Orange County, CALIFORNIA, founded in 1776. Swallows that nest in its ruins are believed to fly south each year on St. John's Day (October 23) and return the following spring on March 19 (St. Joseph's Day).

**San Simeon** the CALIFORNIA mansion of WILLIAM RANDOLPH HEARST. It is a major tourist attraction.

**Sandburg, Carl** 1878–1967. Biographer and poet. Sandburg was treasured as the unofficial national poet. His poetic works were collected in *The Complete Poems* (1950), which won him a PULITZER PRIZE. Among his biographies is the six-volume *Abraham Lincoln* (1926–1939).

**Santa Claus** popularized version of St. Nicholas, a legendary Christian saint who distributed gifts at Christmas. In the modern version, he is believed to reside at the North Pole along with his elves and his reindeer.

**Santa Fe Trail** former commercial route to the West starting in western MISSOURI and ending at Santa Fe in NEW MEXICO, a distance of about 800 miles.

**Sargent, John Singer** 1856–1925. Painter. Sargent is noted for his portraits of beautiful women and children and fashionable personalities. He also did a number of murals, especially for the Boston Public Library.

**Saroyan, William** 1908–1981. Writer. His best-known works include his 1934 anthology *The Daring Young Men on the Flying Trapeze*, his novel *The Human Comedy* (1942), and his play *The Time of Your Life*, which won the PULITZER PRIZE in 1940.

**sarsaparilla** 1. a tropical plant whose roots are used to make a flavorful extract. 2. the extract from the root of the sarsaparilla. 3. a drink flavored with sarsaparilla.

**Sasquatch** a large and hairy creature of folklore, believed to exist in the Pacific Northwest. Also called *bigfoot*.

**SAT** SCHOLASTIC APTITUDE TEST.

**Satchmo** LOUIS ARMSTRONG.

*Saturday Evening Post* one of the most popular general interest magazines, founded in 1821. Its heyday was under editor George H. Lorimer (1899–1936).

**SC** SOUTH CAROLINA. (The official two-letter post office abbreviation.)

**Scarface** AL CAPONE.

**Schlesinger, Arthur Meier, Jr.** 1917–. Historian. He won two PULITZER PRIZES, for *The Age of Jackson* (1946) and *A Thousand Days: John F. Kennedy in the White House* (1965). As a leading spokesman for liberal causes, he was also one of the founders of Americans for Democratic Action.

**Schoenberg, Arnold Franz Walter** 1874–1951. Composer. Austrian-born Schoenberg's main legacy to the musical world was his invention of the 12-tone technique, a new and controversial musical language.

**Scholastic Aptitude Test** a standardized exam required by many colleges for admission. It tests verbal and mathematical ability. Abbreviated SAT.

**Scientology** a pseudoreligious cult based on the psychological theories of science fiction writer, L. Ron Hubbard.

**scifi** science fiction, a literary genre dealing with technological exploits or scientific discoveries.

**Scopes Trial** the trial in Dayton, TENNESSEE, in 1925 pitting Christian fundamentalists against the Darwinian evolutionists. The defendant, a schoolteacher named John T. Scopes, accused of violating a state law against the teaching of evolution in schools, was defended by CLARENCE DARROW, and the fundamentalist cause was pleaded by WILLIAM JENNINGS BRYAN. Scopes was convicted. Also known as the *Monkey Trial*.

**Scrabble** the trademarked name of a board game resembling a crossword puzzle. Devised in the 1930s by Alfred M. Butts, an unemployed architect.

**scrapple** CORNMEAL MUSH, pork, and spices made into a loaf, cut into slices, and fried.

**scrimshaw** carved or engraved whalebone or ivory.

**SD** SOUTH DAKOTA. (The official two-letter post office abbreviation.)

**Sea World** a THEME PARK located in several states that features large aquariums and performing dolphins and other sea creatures. Locations include Orlando, FLORIDA; San Diego, CALIFORNIA; San Antonio, TEXAS; and near Cleveland, OHIO.

**Sears** Trademark. Sears, Roebuck, and Company, a major department store chain founded by Richard Sears (1862–1914) and Alvah Roebuck (1863–1948) as a mail-order business in 1893.

**Sears Tower** a skyscraper located in Chicago, ILLINOIS. Completed in 1973, it stands 1,454 feet tall, and was for many years the world's tallest building. Its offices were originally occupied by SEARS employees.

**SEC** Securities and Exchange Commission.

**Second Awakening** the Great Revival.

**second lady** the wife of the vice president of the United States.

**secondhand smoke** smoke inhaled by nonsmokers from proximity to smokers. Also called *passive smoke*.

**Secret Service** a branch of the U.S. Department of the Treasury responsible for guarding the president and vice president and their families as well as presidential candidates and visiting foreign officials.

**Securities and Exchange Commission** a federal agency established in 1934 that enforces federal laws concerning buying and selling stocks and bonds. It also investigates complaints and regulates national stock exchanges. Abbreviated SEC.

**Seeger, Pete** 1919–. Folk singer. Seeger has been associated since the 1930s with radical causes. Among his best-known folk songs are the antiwar anthem "Where Have All the Flowers Gone" and "Turn, Turn, Turn."

**self-serve** describing a type of store, restaurant, gas station, etc., where customers serve themselves rather than being helped by an employee.

**Seminole** Native American people, one of the Five Civilized Tribes, who were forced out of their original home in Florida in the mid-19th century.

**Semper Fidelis** Latin, "always faithful." Motto of the U.S. Marine Corps.

**Senate** the upper house of Congress, made up of two senators from each state. The vice president presides over the Senate.

**senator** a member of the Senate. Senators are elected by the voters in the state they represent and serve six-year terms. They must meet age, residency, and citizenship requirements.

**Sendak, Maurice** 1928–. Illustrator and author of children's books. He is the first American to win the coveted Hans Christian Andersen Award.

**Seneca Falls Convention**  the first women's rights convention, held in Seneca Falls, NEW YORK, in 1848.

**senior citizen**  a person over the age of 65 or past the age of retirement.

**Sennett, Mack**  1884–1960. Film director and producer. Sennett created the KEYSTONE KOPS and purveyed slapstick comedy during the early years of the cinema.

**sequoia**  either of two species of giant evergreen trees found near the Pacific coast of the United States. One species, the redwood, grows up to 340 feet high and has a trunk up to 25 feet in diameter.

**serial killer**  a psychopath who murders people in a predictable homicidal pattern with similar weapons after luring victims in the same fashion.

**serial marriage**  a series of successive but temporary marriages.

**Serra, Junipero**  1713–1784. Roman Catholic Franciscan missionary. Serra founded eight CALIFORNIA missions, including San Diego in 1769.

*Sesame Street*  a popular educational television show for preschool children, which premiered in 1969.

**Seton, Elizabeth Ann Bayley**  1774–1821. Roman Catholic saint. Seton was the first native-born American to be canonized as a saint. She also founded the first American sisterhood, the Daughters of Charity of Vincent de Paul.

**Seven Sisters**  a consortium of women's colleges established in 1915 and now consisting of Mount Holyoke, Vassar, Wellesley, Smith, Bryn Mawr, Barnard, and Radcliffe.

**Seward's Folly**  the 1867 purchase of ALASKA from the Russian government by William Henry Seward (1801–1872), secretary of state from 1861 to 1869. The price of over $7 million for the land was seen by many as foolish.

**sexism**  prejudice on the basis of gender, especially discrimination against women.

**sexual harrassment** a criminal offense involving unwelcome sexual advances or sexist practices that cause emotional distress.

**Shakers** a millenarian religious sect founded in England around 1750 as an offshoot of the Quakers and brought to the United States in 1774. They were called Shakers because of their ecstatic body movements during worship. They practiced celibacy and communal living with full equality of property and were noted for the elegant and simple style of their furniture.

**shareware** software distributed free of charge.

**shark repellent** a set of financial mechanisms used by a corporation to deter corporate raiders.

**sheriff** the top law enforcement officer in a COUNTY.

**Sherwood, Robert Emmel** 1896–1955. Editor and playwright. Sherwood was a socially conscious playwright best known for *The Petrified Forest* (1935), *Idiot's Delight* (1936), and *Abe Lincoln in Illinois* (1938), each of which won a PULITZER PRIZE.

**shield law** a law that protects the confidentiality of information acquired by journalists in the course of their investigation or reporting.

**shindig** a loud dance, party, or other celebration.

**Shirley Temple** a nonalcoholic drink, generally made with lemon-lime soda or ginger ale, served to underage children in restaurants. Named for the child actress of the same name.

**shopping center** MALL.

**shopping mall** MALL.

**Show-Me State** MISSOURI.

**shunpike** a side road that runs close to an expressway or turnpike but has no tolls.

**sick building syndrome** a set of symptoms, such as eye or skin irritation, sore throat, headache, nausea, and dizziness, affecting persons living or working in polluted buildings.

**sierra** a mountain range with an irregular outline.

**Sierra Nevada** an eastern CALIFORNIA mountain range.

**significant other** a spouse or partner.

**silent generation** the generation that came of age in the 1950s, considered as conformist and complacent, especially in contrast to the very vocal generation that dominated the 1960s.

**silent majority** the politically inactive middle class whose voice on the great issues of the day is drowned out by the more vocal minority.

**silent spring** the degradation or extinction of bird and animal life as a result of the widespread use of toxic chemicals in the environment. From the title of the 1962 book by RACHEL CARSON, ecologist.

**Silicon Valley** region in northern CALIFORNIA where the electronic and computer manufacturing industries are concentrated.

**Silver State** NEVADA.

**Simon, Neil** 1927–. Playwright. Simon is best known for his sophisticated comedies, which include *Barefoot in the Park* (1963) and *The Odd Couple* (1965).

**sin tax** a tax levied on activities generally regarded as sinful or harmful, such as gambling, alcohol, and tobacco.

**Sinatra, Frank** 1915–. Singer and actor. One of the most successful male vocalists of the 20th century. In a career spanning more than 60 years he has had more than 100 hit singles and has also appeared in more than 50 films. Among the many nicknames by which he is known to his devoted fans are *The Voice, Old Blue Eyes,* and *Chairman of the Board.* He won an ACADEMY AWARD for his performance in *From Here to Eternity* (1953).

**Sinclair, Upton** 1878–1968. Novelist. Known as a MUCKRAKER, Sinclair wrote passionately socialist works including *The Jungle* (1906).

**Sing Sing** a state prison located in Ossining, NEW YORK.

**Sioux** NATIVE AMERICANS of the GREAT PLAINS, including the Lakota, the Dakota, and the Nakota, noted as buffalo hunters and horsemen.

**Sisterhood** the women's movement as a whole or any significant group in it considered as a source of mutual support and bonding for women.

**sitcom** a situation comedy, a genre of television comedies based on domestic misadventures.

**Sitting Bull** c1834–1890. SIOUX chief. In 1876, Sitting Bull led the Sioux in the Battle of the Little Bighorn, which resulted in the defeat of General GEORGE ARMSTRONG CUSTER (1839–1876) and his cavalry. He later appeared in the WILD WEST SHOW and was killed at WOUNDED KNEE.

**situation ethics** a form of ethics that holds that absolute ethical rules or religious commandments cannot be binding in certain special situations where extenuating circumstances blur the distinction between right and wrong.

**Six Flags** a large THEME PARK company that owns twelve parks in eight locations across the United States. Known for their thrill rides, the parks also showcase characters from WARNER BROTHERS cartoons.

**skid row** an urban area of run-down bars and hotels that is frequented by derelicts and vagrants.

**skinhead** a working-class bigot with fascist sympathies, generally with close-cropped hair and hobnailed boots who bullies and harasses weaker persons of minority groups.

**Skinner, B. F.** 1904–1990. Psychologist. Skinner devised controversial psychological concepts and techniques, such as operant conditioning and behavior modification through positive and negative reinforcements.

**sky marshal** a federal law enforcement official assigned to protect aircraft, airports, and air passengers.

**slam-dunk** in BASKETBALL, when a player forcefully throws the ball into the net from high above, ensuring a goal.

**slate** the digital board held in front of a camera identifying the shot numbers, director, camera crew, studio, and title. So called because it was originally written on with a chalk.

**Sloan, John** See Ashcan School.

**sloppy joe** a round bun covered with a sauce of ground beef, tomatoes, and seasonings. So called because the filling often falls from the bun as one eats it.

**slush fund** political contributions received by a candidate from dubious sources or for which there is no proper accounting.

**smart car** a futuristic car with computer and video screen on the dashboard capable of guiding the driver to the proper destination.

**smiley** See emoticon.

**Smith, Alfred E.** See Happy Warrior.

**Smith, Bessie** 1894–1937. Singer. Known as the Empress of the Blues, Smith left a mark on the blues with her passionate delivery and rich voice.

**Smith, John** c1580–1631. Colonist. Leader of the Jamestown colony in Virginia. He mapped Virginia and New England and wrote a history of English settlements in the region.

**Smith, Joseph** 1805–1844. Mormon leader. Founder of the Church of Jesus Christ of Latter-day Saints. He published the core doctrinal works on which the Mormon religion is based, including *The Book of Mormon* (1830) and *Doctrine and Covenants* (1835).

**Smithsonian Institution** a famous Washington, D.C., scientific institute composed of several museums, including the National Gallery of Art and the National Air and Space Museum. It was founded in 1846 by an act of Congress utilizing the bequest of James Smithson (1765–1829), an English chemist and benefactor.

**smokey** a state trooper patrolling a highway. From the type of wide-brimmed hat worn by state troopers resembling the forest-ranger hat of Smokey the Bear.

**Smokey the Bear** a public relations symbol of the U.S. Forest Service, used in campaigns against forest fires.

**smoking gun** decisive and incontrovertible evidence. From fictional situations in which the ideal evidence of a homicide is a recently fired gun in the hands of the murderer.

**Smoky Mountains** part of the APPALACHIAN MOUNTAINS that lie in NORTH CAROLINA and TENNESSEE.

**SNCC** Student Nonviolent Coordinating Committee, a civil rights organization of the 1960s that later broke away from more moderate black groups to espouse radical black power.

**Snow Belt** the northern region of the United States extending from MAINE to MONTANA, which experiences the most snowfall in the winter season.

**soap opera** any serial episodic television drama presented mostly in daytime, so called because it was originally sponsored by soap companies. It follows the lives and loves of multiple characters over many years. Also called *soap*.

**soapbox racing** a competition in which unpowered vehicles, made in the early days of soapboxes, raced down inclined tracks.

**soca** West Indian music blending SOUL MUSIC and CALYPSO.

**soccer mom** a suburban housewife who is caught up in the chores of bringing up kids and caring for the family and who takes a strong interest in politics.

**Social Security** a federal program that provides income to the elderly, unemployed, poor, injured, disabled, etc. Introduced as part of the NEW DEAL legislation, it is funded by payroll taxes paid by employees and employers.

**Social Security Administration** an agency within the United States DEPARTMENT OF HEALTH AND HUMAN SERVICES that administers Social Security benefits to the retired, disabled, the families of wage earners who have died, etc. Abbreviated SSA.

**Social Security number** a unique number assigned to each U.S. citizen by the SOCIAL SECURITY ADMINISTRATION. Abbreviated SSN.

**sod hut** an early kind of dwelling built by settlers on the GREAT PLAINS.

**sodbuster** a pioneer farmer who first plowed the soil of the GREAT PLAINS.

**soft science** any of the behavioral or social sciences, such as economics, politics, sociology, and psychology. Distinguished from HARD SCIENCE.

**softball** 1. a game similar to BASEBALL that is played with a bigger, softer ball. 2. the ball used in the game of softball.

**softgel** a hermetically sealed pill containing a medication in a liquid or semisolid state.

**soho** 1. small office/home office, an office maintained by a small entrepreneur in his or her home. 2. Capitalized: a region in New York City noted as the center of avant-garde culture.

**Son of Sam law** law in force in some states that prohibits convicted criminals from making money by selling their stories to the media.

**Sondheim, Stephen** 1930–. Composer. Creator of haunting songs for the conventional musical theatre, Sondheim wrote the lyrics for such classics as *A Funny Thing Happened on the Way to the Forum* (1962) and *West Side Story* (1957).

**Sonoran Desert** a large desert covering southwestern ARIZONA, southeastern CALIFORNIA, and northwestern Mexico. Its native plants include the MESQUITE and the SAGUARO CACTUS.

**Sooner State** OKLAHOMA.

**soul** the essence of black experience in terms of both its emotional intensity and its authenticity. The term also expresses black pride and black spirit as distinct from that of whites and other races. Used in conjunction with other words, as in soul food, SOUL MUSIC, soul brother.

**soul music** a blend of RHYTHM AND BLUES and GOSPEL MUSIC, evocative of the spiritual roots of AFRICAN-AMERICAN music.

**sound bite** a brief television or radio segment that presents bits and pieces from long speeches or statements more for dramatic effect than for fidelity to truth.

**sourdough** a prospector, especially during the KLONDIKE GOLD RUSH.

**Sousa, John Philip** 1854–1932. Composer of marching tunes. Known as the March King, Sousa wrote 136 marches, of which the best known are "Semper Fidelis" (1888) and "The Stars and Stripes Forever" (1897).

**South** 1. the southern states of the United States; the CONFEDERACY. Compare NORTH. 2. generic term for the developing countries of Asia, Africa, and Latin America. Compare NORTH. Also, THIRD WORLD.

**South Carolina** a state in the southeastern United States, known as the Palmetto State. Its capital and largest city is Columbia. The Carolina yellow jessamine is the state flower, and the Carolina wren is the state bird. Abbreviated SC.

**South Dakota** a state in the northern United States. Known as the Coyote State, its capital is Pierre and its largest city is Sioux Falls. The ringnecked pheasant is the state bird, and the American pasqueflower is the state flower. Abbreviated SD.

**Southern belle** an attractive and admired young lady belonging to the family of a typical plantation owner in the old SOUTH.

**spaghetti western** a WESTERN made in Italy with a higher level of violence than found in American westerns.

**spam** to post inappropriate messages on the INTERNET or to send unsolicited junk E-MAIL to newsgroups.

**Spanglish** a mixture of Spanish and English widely spoken in the southwestern United States with large Hispanic communities.

**Spanish-American War** 1898 war against Spain, the chief purpose of which was to liberate Cuba from Spanish control. As a result, Cuba gained its independence and the United States won GUAM, the Philippines, and PUERTO RICO.

**speakeasy** an illegal bar during the PROHIBITION era. So called because customers tended to speak in hushed tones.

**speed bump** a raised ridge across a road near a school or other public facility designed to make drivers brake their vehicles and slow down.

**speed metal** a loud and fast form of HEAVY METAL music.

**spelling bee** See BEE.

**spin doctor** a public relations expert or press agent who reinterprets the news with a new slant to suit the image of his or her client.

***Spirit of St. Louis, The*** the monoplane CHARLES LINDBERGH used to fly nonstop across the Atlantic.

**spiritual** an AFRICAN-AMERICAN religious musical genre that evolved during slavery. Also called Negro spiritual, it expressed a plaintive homesickness for heaven and sorrow over present misery. The BLUES was directly descended from spirituals.

The Spirit of St. Louis

**Spock, Benjamin McLane** 1903–. Pediatrician. Author of the bestselling *Common Sense Book of Baby and Child Care* (1946), a controversial book on child rearing and disciplining. In the 1960s he became active in the peace movement.

**spoiler party** a minor party that contests an election not with hopes of winning but only to hurt the chances of either of the top contestants. Also, called *third party*.

**spoils system** a system of political patronage by which civil service jobs and contracts are used as rewards for the followers of a successful political candidate.

**spoon bread** a baked bread dish made with cornmeal, shortening, and eggs. It is usually served from its baking container with a spoon.

**spork** blend of *spoon* and *fork*. A plastic spoon with blunt tines that can be used as a fork. It is usually found in fast-food restaurants.

**sports drink**  a noncarbonated drink designed to replenish energy and boost the stamina of athletes.

**Spud State**  IDAHO, known for its potato crops.

**square dance**  a folk dance in which four couples forming a square perform designated steps.

**Square Deal**  THEODORE ROOSEVELT's name for his reform program.

**SRO hotel**  single-room occupancy hotel, usually inhabited by poor and indigent people on welfare.

**SSA**  SOCIAL SECURITY ADMINISTRATION.

**SSN**  SOCIAL SECURITY NUMBER.

**St. Patrick's Cathedral**  the largest Roman Catholic cathedral in the United States, built on Fifth Avenue in New York City between 1858 and 1879 and designed by JAMES RENWICK.

**St. Valentine's Day Massacre**  February 14, 1929, execution-style killing in Chicago, ILLINOIS. Seven members of the Moran gang, a rival of AL CAPONE's, were lined up against a wall and shot. Capone ordered the killing.

**stagecoach**  a four-wheeled, horse-drawn vehicle that carried long-distance mail, freight, and passengers in prerailroad days. So called because it covered distances in stages.

**Stanton, Elizabeth Cady**  1815–1902. Women's rights advocate. She organized the SENECA FALLS CONVENTION, the first woman's rights convention, in 1848 and served as first president of National Women Suffrage Association.

**"Star Spangled Banner"**  the national anthem of the United States. The lyrics were written by Francis Scott Key, and it is set to the music of an old English song, "To Anacreon in Heaven." It was adopted as the national anthem by CONGRESS in 1931.

**Stars and Bars**  the CONFEDERATE flag. It consists of a blue and a white cross on a red field on which is superimposed a cross of white stars.

**Stars and Stripes** the national flag of the United States, with 13 stripes and 50 stars.

**State Department** DEPARTMENT OF STATE.

**State of the Union Address** an annual address delivered to both houses of CONGRESS by the president every January, outlining the administration's program for the coming year. It is required by the Constitution.

*Stars and Bars*

**Statue of Liberty** a large statue depicting liberty as a woman holding a book and a flaming torch, designed by French sculptor Frederic Bartholdi (1834–1904). Located on Liberty Island in New York City's harbor, it was presented to the U.S. government by the French government to commemorate the centennial of U.S. independence.

**status offender** a juvenile who is classified as a delinquent because of unruliness or incorrigibility.

**Stealth bomber** a high-tech military plane sheathed in radar-absorbing materials, designed to elude radar detection.

**Steffens, Lincoln, Jr.** 1866–1936. Journalist and author. Steffens was a MUCKRAKER who exposed the corruption of city officials in *The Shame of the Cities* (1904) and other books.

**Steichen, Edward** 1879–1983. Photographer. Associate of ALFRED STIEGLITZ, he headed the photography section of New York Museum of Modern Art (MOMA) and organized its *Family of Man* exhibit in 1955.

**Stein, Gertude** 1874–1946. Novelist. Stein is best known as the nurturer of other creative talents, such as ERNEST HEMINGWAY, and as an epigrammatist. Her Paris apartment became a salon for the literary intelligentsia and expatriates. Her literary style was heavily experimental, influenced by Picasso's Cubism.

**Steinbeck, John** 1902–1968. Writer. Steinbeck celebrated the struggle of the human spirit against the dehumanization of society and the corruption of greed. His reputation was established in *Tortilla Flat* (1935), and he developed similar themes in *Of Mice and Men* (1937) and *The Grapes of Wrath* (1939). He won the Nobel Prize for Literature in 1962.

**Stetson** a trademarked name for a broad-brimmed, high-peaked hat popular with cowboys and in WESTERNS. From John B. Stetson (1830–1905), Philadelphia hatmaker.

**sticker shock** the shock experienced by potential buyers over sticker prices far higher than they had anticipated.

**Stieglitz, Alfred** 1864–1946. Photographer. He helped to transform photography into a serious art form. Stieglitz was the mentor of many great photographers, including EDWARD STEICHEN, whose work he showcased in his journals, *Camera Notes* and *Camera Work*.

**sting** a law enforcement operation designed to entrap offenders by offering them the necessary bait or inducement.

**stonewall** to foil any investigation by obstinate silence or obstructionist tactics.

**storyboard** the rough sketches showing the plot, action, and characters of a film in proper sequence.

**Stowe, Harriet Beecher** 1811–1896. Author of *Uncle Tom's Cabin*, a powerful antislavery novel. Like her father Lyman Beecher (1775–1863) and brother Henry Ward Beecher (1813–1887), she was a staunch abolitionist.

**straight-arrow** a morally upright person whose actions are above reproach.

**Stravinsky, Igor Fedorovich** 1882–1971. Composer. One of the titans of 20th century music, Stravinsky's extraordinary sense of rhythm and timbre enabled him to improvise boldly throughout his career. He combined elements of classical music, Russian musical idioms, and rhythms from the BIG BANDS. Among his best-known works are *Les Noces* (1923) and *The Rake's Progress* (1951).

**streetcar** a large passenger vehicle that travels on rails on the street and is powered by electricity.

**strip city** a long, narrow stretch of urban development between two larger cities.

**strip mall** a group of stores arranged in a line, usually with parking spaces in front of each store.

**Strip, The** a stretch of famous hotels and casinos along Las Vegas Boulevard in LAS VEGAS, NEVADA.

**sub(marine sandwich)** a sandwich on a long bread roll. Also called *hero, hoagie, grinder,* or *poorboy,* depending on the area of the country.

**succotash** a dish of cooked corn and beans.

**Sullivan, Louis** 1856–1924. Architect. Forerunner of FRANK LLOYD WRIGHT, Sullivan was a major force in the development of high-rise commercial buildings and the introduction of rich, abstract ornamentation. Among his more notable buildings are the Auditorium Building in Chicago, ILLINOIS, the Wainwright Building in St. Louis, MISSOURI, and the Guaranty Trust Building in Buffalo, NEW YORK.

**Sultan of Swat** BABE RUTH.

**summer stock** repertory theater that is performed during the summer.

**Sun Belt** the southern and southwestern United States, especially states that have a warmer climate for most of the year.

**sun dance** a dance ceremony performed by Plains Indians to induce states of trance. In some cases, the dancers were hooked by thongs to a central pole and forced to bleed.

**Sunflower State** KANSAS.

**sunset law** a law obligating government agencies to justify their continued existence through an overall assessment of their functions, goals, and effectiveness.

**Sunshine State** FLORIDA.

**Super Bowl** the biggest event in the annual FOOTBALL season, in which the champions of the NATIONAL FOOTBALL LEAGUE and the AMERICAN FOOTBALL CONFERENCE meet for a final deciding game.

**Superman** a comic book hero, created by Joe Shuster and Jerry Siegel, who could perform feats of prodigious strength and also fly and see through solid objects.

**supertitle** a written translation of the dialogue or lyrics of a foreign language opera or chorale displayed on a screen.

**supply-side** an economic policy that advocates increasing the supply of goods, rather than stimulating the demand for them, in order to boost the economy and increase employment. Compare DEMAND-SIDE.

**Supreme Court** the highest court of the United States, established by the Third Article of the CONSTITUTION. It consists of a Chief Justice and eight associate justices. Justices are appointed by the president and confirmed by the Senate, and serve for life. Landmark Supreme Court decisions include *BROWN V. BOARD OF EDUCATION* and *ROE V. WADE*.

**Swamp Fox** nickname of REVOLUTIONARY WAR hero, Francis Marion (1732–1795).

**SWAT** Special Weapons And Tactics team, a crack commando strike force assigned to dangerous missions, such as a hostage situation.

**sweeps** the month-long periods, usually in February, May, July and November, when Nielsen Media Research measures audiences in all television markets.

**swing** rhythmic ballroom dance music popular from the 1930s to the 1950s. Played by the BIG BANDS, its strongest element was JAZZ.

**Tabasco sauce**  a trademarked brand of sauce made of spicy hot peppers.

**tabloid**  a daily or weekly newspaper with a smaller page format than a regular newspaper and containing more sensational reporting.

**taco**  a folded soft or crispy tortilla filled with food, usually meat, cheese, chopped tomatoes, and shredded lettuce. A TEX-MEX food.

**taffy**  a chewy candy made from molasses or sugar that is boiled down.

**Taft, William Howard**  1857–1930. Twenty-seventh president of the United States (1909–1913). Taft was chief justice of the SUPREME COURT from 1921–1930.

**tag sale**  a YARD SALE.

**take**  the filming of a shot in a particular camera setting.

**take-no-prisoners**  adopting a highly punitive and uncompromising attitude toward opponents.

**talk show**  a television show in which the host entertains viewers by interviewing colorful guests.

**Tammany Hall**  the nickname for the Democratic political machine in New York City. Founded in 1789 as the Society of Tammany, it became under WILLIAM MARCY "BOSS" TWEED a hotbed for corruption.

**tap dancing** form of step dancing where the dancer wears shoes with metal plates or taps to accentuate the rhythm. It was a staple of VAUDEVILLE.

**Tarheel State** NORTH CAROLINA.

**Tarzan** a fictional character created by author EDGAR RICE BURROUGHS. As a child Tarzan was abandoned in the African bush and raised by apes.

**Tax Day** April 15, the final date for submitting tax returns to the INTERNAL REVENUE SERVICE each year.

**tax shelter** a failed investment or other legal mechanisms used to avoid or reduce one's income tax liability.

**Taylor, Zachary** 1784–1850. Twelfth president of the United States (1849–1850). His nickname was *Old Rough and Ready*. Taylor became ill and died in office.

**Teamsters** a labor union, mainly of truckers, considered one of the most powerful in the United States.

**Teapot Dome Scandal** a political scandal during the administration of President WARREN G. HARDING, in which Interior Secretary Albert Fall accepted bribes from developers of Teapot Dome, a federal oil reserve in WYOMING.

**teaser** an attention-grabbing segment of a television program presented at the start of a show to attract viewers.

**techie** a student in a technical institute.

**technology assessment** an evaluation of the potential or possible impact of new technologies, especially its social costs, effects on the workforce, and environmental consequences.

**technology transfer** the transfer of technical know-how from advanced to less developed countries or from experimental or publicly funded agencies to the private sector.

**Tecumseh** 1768–1813. Shawnee leader. He was defeated by U.S. forces at the Battle of Tippecanoe in 1811 and sided with the British in the WAR OF 1812.

**teddy bear**  a stuffed toy bear. Named for THEODORE ROOSEVELT, who was often called "Teddy."

**telecommute**  to work at home while maintaining contacts with a main office through a computer and modem.

**telemedicine**  medical diagnosis and consultation by electronic means such as phone, video, and computers.

**TelePrompter**  a trademarked device used in television that provides an entertainer with an enlarged line-by-line reproduction of a script outside the range of an audience's vision.

**televangelist**  a Christian evangelist who preaches regularly to large television audiences.

**television ratings**  a ratings system developed in response to viewers' concerns about increasing violence and sex on television. Ratings are designed to help parents decide which shows are appropriate for their children. The ratings codes are similar to those for movies. (See MOVIE RATINGS.)

**temperance movement**  a national movement beginning in the early 1800s for the banning of alcohol. It gained strength through the efforts of women suffragists. Its greatest success was the passage of the Eighteenth Amendment, making PROHIBITION the law of the land.

**Temple Black, Shirley**  1928–. Actress. Temple was an extremely popular child actress of the 1930s whose films included *Dimples* and *Wee Willie Winkie*. Later in life she entered politics, becoming the U.S. ambassador to Ghana.

**tenderfoot**  in COWBOY lingo, a novice, not used to rough living and hardships.

**tenderloin**  an area or police precinct that affords the most opportunity for graft.

**Tennessee**  a state in the southern United States. Called the Volunteer State, its capital is Nashville and its largest city is Memphis. The iris is the state flower, and the mockingbird is the state bird. Abbreviated TN.

**Tennessee Valley Authority** a government corporation established to promote and stimulate economic growth in the Tennessee Valley area. Abbreviated TVA.

**tent pole** a television program that is so popular that the audience stays to watch the succeeding shows.

**term limits** limits set by law on the number of terms that a popularly elected legislator can serve in a legislature.

**TESL** teaching of English as a second language.

**TESOL** 1. teaching English to speakers of other languages. 2. teachers of English to speakers of other languages. A national organization dedicated to the advancement of the teaching of English as a second language.

**Texas** a state in the southern United States that borders Mexico. Known as the Lone Star State, its capital is Austin and its largest city is Houston. The mockingbird is the state bird, and the bluebonnet is the state flower. Texas was an independent republic from 1836–1845. Abbreviated TX.

**Texas longhorn** a breed of long-horned domestic cattle from the U.S. Southwest.

**Texas Rangers** a volunteer home guard formed in the 1820s against Indian attacks. It gradually evolved into a frontier militia.

**Tex-Mex** music or food that mixes Texan and Mexican elements.

**Thalberg, Irving Grant** 1899–1936. Film producer. Thalberg almost single-handedly made MGM the most powerful studio in HOLLYWOOD, producing a number of classics, such as *Ben-Hur* (1925), *Anna Christie* (1930), *Mutiny on the Bounty* (1935), and *The Good Earth* (1937).

**Thanksgiving** an American harvest holiday, celebrated as a national holiday since 1863 on the last Thursday in November. The first Thanksgiving was a 1621 feast held by the PILGRIMS in the PLYMOUTH COLONY to celebrate their survival of the first year in the NEW WORLD.

**theme park** an amusement park organized around a single theme, such as wildlife, science, or fairy tales.

**think tank** an institute, generally funded through philanthropic contributions, in which several dedicated researchers and scholars are employed to think, research, and publish.

**Third World** the less-developed countries of the world, considered as a bloc, distinct from the FIRST WORLD.

**thirteen colonies** the original thirteen colonies of the United States: CONNECTICUT, DELAWARE, GEORGIA, MARYLAND, MASSACHUSETTS, NEW HAMPSHIRE, NEW JERSEY, NEW YORK, NORTH CAROLINA, PENNSYLVANIA, RHODE ISLAND, SOUTH CAROLINA, and VIRGINIA.

**Thoreau, Henry David** 1817–1862. Essayist and philosopher of radical humanism. Highly individualistic, Thoreau is noted for his two-year retreat from civilization that resulted in the book *Walden* (1854), and for his promotion of civil disobedience placing conscience over his duties as a citizen.

**thread** a series of related messages in a newsgroup.

**Three Stooges** a comedy trio, originally consisting of Moe Howard, Shemp Howard, and Larry Fine, whose slapstick was marked by brainless banter. Performing under the names Moe, Curly, and Larry, the Three Stooges appeared in several successful films in the 1930s.

**Three-Mile Island** an island near Harrisburg, PENNSYLVANIA, the site of a 1979 accident at a nuclear power plant that resulted in radiation being released, contaminating the surrounding area.

**Thurber, James** 1894–1961. Writer. Thurber's pieces for the *The New Yorker*, often illustrated by his own acerbic cartoons, skewered the follies of modern life with a unique brand of humor.

**Tiffany** decorative Art Nouveau glass designs created by Louis Comfort Tiffany (1848–1933).

*Time* news magazine founded in 1923 by HENRY LUCE and Briton Hadden.

**time warp** a discontinuity or distortion in the sequence of events on a timeline.

**timeline** a chart showing historical events in their proper chronological sequence.

**Times Square** the theater and entertainment area at the intersection of Broadway and Seventh Avenues in central MANHATTAN. It is the site of a popular New Year's Eve celebration each year.

**Tin Lizzie** nickname of the MODEL T Ford. Probably from tin limousine.

**Tin Pan Alley** a metaphor for the commercial music industry in the early part of the 20th century. From Tin Pan, an area in New York City around West 28th Street where most of the music publishers were located.

**Tinseltown** HOLLYWOOD.

**Titanic** a giant luxury ship that hit an iceberg and sank in the Atlantic Ocean in 1912 on its maiden voyage from London to NEW YORK. Over 1,500 passengers perished in this tragedy, perhaps the most written about maritime disaster in modern history.

**Tlingit** people native to ALASKA, who are mostly boatbuilders, wood-carvers, and weavers.

**TN** TENNESSEE. (The official two-letter post office abbreviation.)

**TOEFL** testing of English as a foreign language. A standardized test to determine the fluency in English of a nonnative speaker of English. It is required by many universities for admission of foreign students.

**toll road** a road on which drivers must pay a toll to travel. The toll is usually paid at a TOLLBOOTH or tollgate on the road. Funds collected from such roads are usually used to pay for their maintenance. Also called a *tollway*.

**tollbooth** a place where a fee or toll is collected from vehicles using a TOLL ROAD or toll bridge.

**tollway** a TOLL ROAD.

**Tom Thumb, General** the stage name of Charles Stratton (1838–1883), a midget in P.T. Barnum's GREATEST SHOW ON EARTH.

**tomahawk** a NATIVE AMERICAN hatchet or small club used in fighting and hunting.

**Tomb of the Unknown Soldier** a memorial in ARLINGTON NATIONAL CEMETERY dedicated to the unidentified dead in foreign wars of the United States.

**Tony Awards** annual awards, named after theater star Antoinette Perry (1888–1946), given since 1947 to recognize excellence in the theatrical arts.

**top brass** See BRASS.

**Tory** 1. a person who subscribes to a right-of-center political ideology. 2. a colonist who was opposed to secession from Great Britain and the REVOLUTIONARY WAR.

**totem pole** a ceremonial carved post of stacked figures used by the Kwakiutl, Tlingit, and other NATIVE AMERICAN tribes of the Northwest as grave markers and heraldic family memorials.

**touchdown** in FOOTBALL, the act of placing the football behind the goal line of the opposing team, thus scoring six points.

**town house** a one-family home attached to other similar homes by common sidewalls.

**track ball** a computer device like a mouse in which the movement of the cursor on the screen is controlled through rotating a small movable ball in a stationary socket.

*totem pole*

**trade dress** a distinctive mix of colors and shapes that is associated with a particular product, and that may form part of its patent or copyright.

**Trail of Tears** the forced march of the peoples of the FIVE CIVILIZED TRIBES from the fertile plains of the Southeast to inhospitable Indian Territory in OKLAHOMA under the Indian Removal Act of 1830. Thousands died along the way of disease and exhaustion.

**Transcendentalism** a uniquely NEW ENGLAND school of philosophy combining romanticism and natural theology, founded by a group of intellectuals including RALPH WALDO EMERSON, SARAH MARGARET FULLER, and HENRY DAVID THOREAU.

**trap** a stage door that allows actors to enter and exit through the stage's floor.

**Treasure State** MONTANA.

**Trekkie** a fan of the science fiction television series, *Star Trek*.

**triage** the efficient allocation of scarce resources in an emergency or crisis, based on practical or utilitarian criteria rather than on humanitarian ones. Compare LIFEBOAT ETHICS.

**triathlon** an athletic event combining running, swimming, and bicycling.

**trick or treat** the greeting used by costumed children when visiting homes on Halloween. They visit homes to get treats like candy.

**Triple Crown** the unofficial trio of classic horse races, especially the KENTUCKY DERBY, the Preakness, and the Belmont Stakes.

**triple witching hour** the last trading hour on one of four Fridays in a year when contracts on stock options, futures, and options on futures expire simultaneously.

**Truman, Harry S.** 1884–1972. Thirty-third president of the United States (1945–1953).

**Truth, Sojourner** c1797–1883. Abolitionist and women's rights champion. A slave born Isabella Baumfree, Truth escaped to freedom, experienced religious conversion, adopted a new name, and then spent the rest of her life as an eloquent advocate of the rights of blacks and women.

**Tubman, Harriet** 1820–1913. Abolitionist. Hailed as the Moses of her people, Tubman helped hundreds of slaves to freedom through the UNDERGROUND RAILROAD.

**tumbleweed** one of several kinds of plants that break from their roots in autumn and tumble around, driven by the wind.

**tunnel vision** a narrow perspective resulting from an excessive focus on the present or on a single idea or activity.

**Turner, Frederick Jackson** 1861–1932. Historian. Turner founded interpretative history with *The Significance of the Frontier in American History*, published in 1920.

**Turner, Nat** 1800–1831. Slave leader. Leader of the most important slave revolt in the United States, Turner was hanged after the revolt was put down.

**turnover** a food item made of a filling folded into a rich crust and baked.

**Tuskegee University** an ALABAMA institution for black studies. Founded in 1881 as the Tuskegee Normal and Industrial Institute, it was one of the first colleges to educate AFRICAN-AMERICANS. GEORGE WASHINGTON CARVER taught there, and BOOKER T. WASHINGTON was once the director of the institute.

**TVA** TENNESSEE VALLEY AUTHORITY.

**Twain, Mark** 1835–1910. Humorist and novelist, born Samuel Langhorne Clemens. He was quintessentially American in his breadth of interests and his exuberance for life. Best known as the creator of *The Adventures of Tom Sawyer* (1876) and *Adventures of Huckleberry Finn* (1884).

*Mark Twain*

**Tweed Ring** See TWEED, WILLIAM MARCY "BOSS".

**Tweed, William Marcy "Boss"** 1823–1878. Politician. Tweed, a powerful TAMMANY

HALL politician, gained complete control of the Democratic Party in New York in the late 19th century through graft and corruption. He and his cohorts, who made up the Tweed Ring, were finally exposed by the *New York Times*.

**12-step program** a program consisting of 12 steps originally adopted by ALCOHOLICS ANONYMOUS for weaning alcoholics from dependence on liquor and helping them to lead normal lives. The program is now used to treat a wide variety of addictions.

**twenty-one** a card game, also known as *blackjack*, in which the players try to accumulate cards with a face value equal to, but not exceeding, 21.

**Twin Cities** the cities of Minneapolis and St. Paul in MINNESOTA.

**TX** TEXAS. (The official two-letter post office abbreviation.)

**Tyler, John** 1790–1862. Tenth president of the United States (1841–1845).

**typhoid Mary** an involuntary carrier of a disease, from nickname of Mary Mallon, an Irish cook in New York City in the 1910s who passed on the typhoid bacterium to dozens of people.

# U

**UFO** unidentified flying object. Unofficial term for objects believed to be of extraterrestrial origin.

**ukulele** a stringed musical instrument similar to a guitar but smaller and with only four strings. It was invented in HAWAII.

**Uncle Sam** personification of the United States, and particularly the federal government. He usually appears in army recruitment posters as a gentleman with a white goatee and top hat. Perhaps from a telegraphic code name for United States.

**Uncle Tom** a servile AFRICAN-AMERICAN who accepts white superiority unquestioningly. Named for the title character in UNCLE TOM'S CABIN.

*Uncle Sam*

***Uncle Tom's Cabin*** an antislavery novel by HARRIET BEECHER STOWE published in 1852. Its influence was so great that ABRAHAM LINCOLN referred to it as "the book that started the great war."

**Underground Railroad** a network of hiding places and escape routes established by abolitionists to bring escaped slaves in the SOUTH to freedom in the NORTH in the days before the CIVIL WAR.

**Union** 1. the United States. 2. the northern states that did not secede from the U.S. government during the CIVIL WAR.

**unisex** applicable to or suitable for both sexes without distinction.

**United States Department of Agriculture** an executive department formed in 1862 to improve farms, conserve natural resources, and inspect and grade the quality of food products. Abbreviated USDA.

**Universal Studios** a large THEME PARK located near Orlando, FLORIDA.

**University of Pennsylvania** an IVY LEAGUE university located in PENNSYLVANIA. Opened in 1751, its chief founder was BENJAMIN FRANKLIN and it started the first university business and medical schools in the country.

**Updike, John** 1932–. Writer. Updike has written many novels, essays, short stories, poems, and book reviews over a course of 40 years, and his prolific output is marked by a deep religious quest for meaning and purpose. He is best known for his novels *Rabbit, Run* and *Rabbit Is Rich*.

**upscale** of or relating to the upper end of a scale of values, income, and social standing.

**upstream** the phase of industrial operation dealing with the initial stages of discovery and production.

**uptown** an area in the upper part of a city; the area away from or opposite of DOWNTOWN.

**upward mobility** the tendency or ability of a person from a lower social class to aspire and move up to a higher class.

**USDA** UNITED STATES DEPARTMENT OF AGRICULTURE.

**Usenet** a collection of networks and computers on the INTERNET organized into newsgroups.

**USO** United Service Organizations, a civilian-run service network catering to military personnel serving overseas.

**UT** UTAH. (The official two-letter post office abbreviation.)

**Utah** a state in the western United States, founded by Mormons. Called the Beehive State, its capital and largest city is Salt Lake City. Its state bird is the California seagull, and its state flower is the sego lily. Abbreviated UT.

# V

**V chip**  an electronic device embedded in a television that blocks programs considered objectionable for children.

**VA**  VIRGINIA. (The official two-letter post office abbreviation.)

**Valentine's Day**  February 14, the day dedicated to St. Valentine, the patron saint of love, when lovers exchange gifts.

**valley of the dolls**  a condition of excessive dependence on stimulants or depressant drugs, commonly known as dolls. From the title of a 1966 novel by Jacqueline Susann.

**Van Buren, Martin**  1782–1862. Eighth president of the United States (1837–1841). He was nicknamed *Old Kinderhook*.

**Vanderbilt, Cornelius**  1794–1877. Businessman. Vanderbilt amassed a great fortune from his railroad holdings and donated $1 million to found Vanderbilt University. The Vanderbilt name is associated with wealth.

**vanity plate**  a custom-made license plate with a name or word or group of numbers selected by the owner.

**variety store**  a store that sells a large selection of inexpensive things.

**vaudeville**  the classic variety theater that flourished between 1890 and 1910 combining all kinds of entertainment, including BURLESQUE, comedy, mime, acrobatics, song, and dance.

**Veblen, Thorstein**  1857–1929. Economist. A leading opponent of conventional economic and social thought, Veblen exposed the economic doctrines of his day in *The Theory of the Leisure Class* (1899) and other books.

**Vermont**  a state in the northeastern United States, known as the Green Mountain State. Its largest city is Burlington, and its capital is Montpelier. The red clover is the state flower, and the hermit thrush is the state bird. Abbreviated VT.

**Vespucci, Amerigo**  1454–1512. Florentine navigator. See AMERICA.

**Veterans Day**  until 1954 called Armistice Day. A holiday on November 11 honoring the veterans of foreign wars.

**Veterans of Foreign Wars**  founded in 1899 after the SPANISH-AMERICAN WAR, it is an organization of U.S. veterans who have served in foreign wars. Abbreviated VFW.

**VFW**  VETERANS OF FOREIGN WARS.

**VI**  the U.S. VIRGIN ISLANDS. (The official two-letter post office abbreviation.)

**victimless crime**  a statutory crime, such as prostitution, pornography, or gambling, that does not inflict physical harm, but rather offends prevailing social mores and standards.

**Vidal, Gore**  1925–. Writer. Cantankerous and controversial, Vidal's many works include historical novels and contemporary social satire.

**videozine**  a combination of a magazine and video; a magazine recorded and circulated as a videocassette.

**Vietnam War**  1954–1975 war between communist North Vietnam and noncommunist South Vietnam. Beginning in the late 1950s, U.S. troops were sent to aid the South Vietnamese, and in the 1960s, more than 500,000 U.S. soldiers were fighting in Vietnam. The war was very unpopular with American citizens, especially HIPPIES, who vigorously protested against it. U.S. troops finally withdrew from Vietnam in 1973, and South Vietnam was overtaken by communists in 1975.

**Vietnam War Memorial**  a memorial in WASHINGTON MALL to the Americans killed during the VIETNAM WAR. The striking monument is a long marble wall covered with the names of those who died.

**Virgin Islands, the U.S.** a U.S. possession composed of nine main islands, the best known of which are St. Croix, St. Thomas, and St. John. Abbreviated VI.

**Virginia** a state in the eastern United States. Known as the Old Dominion State, its capital is Richmond and its largest city is Virginia Beach. The American dogwood is the state flower, and the cardinal is the state bird. Abbreviated VA.

**virtual reality** a computer technology in which hardware and software interact in real time with a user to enable him or her to change the multimedia environment. Generally, the user manipulates the environment with the use of special goggles, stereo headphones, and sensory gloves. Also called *artificial reality*.

**VISTA** Volunteers in Service to America, a domestic peace corps program administered by the federal government.

*Vogue* a fashion magazine founded in 1892.

**voice mail** a computerized telephone service that records messages for later retrieval by a particular recipient.

**Voice, The** FRANK SINATRA.

**voice-over** the recorded voice of an unseen narrator providing a running commentary on the action seen on a television or motion picture screen.

**voiceprinting** a system of personal identification based on sound spectrographs that record patterns of pitch, modulation and inflection in a person's speech.

**Volstead Act** an act of CONGRESS in 1919 that made PROHIBITION official throughout the nation under the Eighteenth Amendment. So called from its sponsor in Congress, Andrew J. Volstead.

**Volunteer State** TENNESSEE.

**voucher plan** conversion of a portion of school tax revenues into redeemable certificates that may be applied toward tuition in private schools.

**VT** VERMONT. (The official two-letter post office abbreviation.)

**WA** WASHINGTON. (The official two-letter post office abbreviation.)

**wake-up call** a call to action on an issue that has been neglected in the past.

**Walden Pond** an idyllic, sylvan place in Concord, MASSACHUSETTS, where HENRY DAVID THOREAU lived from 1845 to 1847.

**Waldorf salad** a salad of chopped apples, celery, walnuts, and mayonnaise. Named for the Waldorf-Astoria hotel in New York City, where it originated.

**Wall Street** a street in New York City where the NEW YORK STOCK EXCHANGE is located. Used metaphorically as a symbol of the financial power of U.S. corporations.

*Wall Street Journal* the best-selling newspaper in the United States and the most influential business daily.

**wall-to-wall** extending from one end to the other, providing total coverage.

**Walt Disney/MGM Studios** one of the three major parks that make up WALT DISNEY WORLD located near Orlando, FLORIDA.

**Walt Disney World** the trademarked name for a large resort and entertainment complex located near Orlando, Florida. It includes THE MAGIC KINGDOM, EPCOT CENTER, WALT DISNEY/MGM STUDIOS, River Country Water Park, Typhoon Lagoon Water Park, Blizzard Beach Water Park, Discovery Island, Pleasure Island, The Disney Institute, and Disney Village Marketplace.

**Walter Mitty** a person who fantasizes as a means of escaping the drab reality of everyday life. From JAMES THURBER's story "The Secret Life of Walter Mitty" (1942).

**wannabe** a person who aspires to be like a role model or celebrity.

**War Between the States** the CIVIL WAR.

**War of 1812** the conflict between the United States and Great Britain between 1812–1815 over shipping rights. Many NATIVE AMERICAN tribes sided with the British in the war, but the United States prevailed.

**War of Secession** the CIVIL WAR.

**Ward, Artemus** 1834–1867. Humorist. Pseudonym of Charles Farrar Browne, whose folksy sayings influenced MARK TWAIN and ABRAHAM LINCOLN.

**Warhol, Andy** 1928–1987. Pop artist. A graphic designer and painter, Warhol produced over 2,000 images that turned trivial and commonplace things into art and art itself into something trivial and commonplace. He is considered the high priest of POP ART.

**Warner Brothers** a movie production company begun by four Warner brothers: Albert (1884–1967), Harry (1881–1958), Jack (1892–1978), and Samuel (1887–1927). They opened their studio in HOLLYWOOD in 1918 and were the first to use synchronized sound in a film.

*Andy Warhol*

**Warren, Robert Penn** 1905–1989. Novelist and poet. Warren is known for his deep Southern consciousness and preoccupation with human dilemmas in a changing society. His best-known novel is *All the King's Men* (1946), a fictional account of Southerner HUEY LONG.

**Washington** a state in the northwestern United States. Called the Evergreen State, its capital is Olympia and its largest city is Seattle. Its state bird is the willow goldfinch, and its state flower is the coast rhododendron. Abbreviated WA.

**Washington, Booker T.** 1856–1915. AFRICAN-AMERICAN educator and champion of vocational training and racial moderation. Washington was president of Tuskegee Institute (now TUSKEGEE UNIVERSITY) from 1881 to 1913. His autobiography, *Up from Slavery*, was published in 1901.

**Washington, D.C.** the capital of the United States.

**Washington, George** 1732–1799. The first president of the United States (1789–1797). Washington was a general in the REVOLUTIONARY WAR, leading his troops to victory against the British in 1781. He is called the *Father of His Country*, and his birthday is a national holiday. See also FOUNDING FATHERS, MOUNT RUSHMORE, and MOUNT VERNON.

*George Washington*

**Washington Mall** a rectangular park in WASHINGTON, D.C. that includes the CAPITOL, the LINCOLN MEMORIAL, the VIETNAM WAR MEMORIAL, and the WASHINGTON MONUMENT. Also called *The Mall*.

**Washington Monument** a tall monument in WASHINGTON MALL honoring GEORGE WASHINGTON. Dedicated in 1888, it is a square, tapered shaft with a pyramid at the top.

**WASP** White Anglo-Saxon Protestant, applied specifically to Protestant Americans of English descent and generally to the white ruling elite.

**Watergate** a 1972 political scandal during the administration of President

*Washington Monument*

RICHARD MILHOUS NIXON that led to his resignation in 1974. The scandal had its origin in a break-in at the Democratic headquarters in the Watergate Hotel complex in WASHINGTON, D. C., a crime in which the president as well as his senior aides were involved directly or indirectly. By extension, any major political scandal.

**Wayne, John** 1907–1979. Actor. Born Marion Michael Morrison, Wayne starred as a tough but warmhearted cowboy in many WESTERNS, winning an OSCAR for his role in *True Grit* (1969).

**WB** a television network owned by WARNER BROTHERS.

**WCTU** WOMEN'S CHRISTIAN TEMPERANCE UNION.

**Webster, Noah** 1758–1843. Lexicographer. The preeminent lexicographer of the United States, Webster has had more influence on American English usage than any other, especially with his *An American Dictionary of the English Language* (1828) and his *Blue-Backed Speller* (1783).

**Weight Watchers** the trademarked name for a group dedicated to helping people lose undesirable weight, usually by strict dieting.

**Welch, Robert H. W.** See JOHN BIRCH SOCIETY.

**Welles, Orson** 1915–1985. Film director and actor. His meteoric rise to fame made him a wunderkind of HOLLYWOOD as the director of an all-time film classic, *Citizen Kane* (1941).

**Wells Fargo** a stagecoach company formed in 1852 by Henry Wells and William Fargo that transported mail and money from the MIDWEST to the West. Now the trademarked name for an armored truck delivery service and electronic security services.

**West, Benjamin** 1738–1820. Quaker painter. West moved to England in 1763, becoming the official history painter to George III and also one of the founders of the Royal Academy.

**West Point** the site of the U.S. Military Academy, the principal training institution for U.S. Army cadets, founded on the banks of the HUDSON RIVER in 1802.

**West Virginia** a state in the southeastern United States. Called the Mountain State, its capital and largest city is Charleston. The rhododendron is its state flower, and the cardinal is its state bird. Abbreviated WV.

**western** a literary and movie genre dealing with the conquest of the West, pitting the good guys against the bad ones, and usually involving battles with NATIVE AMERICANS.

**wetback** a derogatory term for an illegal immigrant from Mexico who enters the United States by swimming across the Rio Grande, the border between the two countries.

**Wharton, Edith** 1862–1937. Novelist. Her most acclaimed novel was *Ethan Frome* (1911), which dealt with the conflicts between individual desires and social conventions.

**Wheat Belt** a region of wheat-producing states. It includes COLORADO, ILLINOIS, KANSAS, MINNESOTA, MISSOURI, MONTANA, NEBRASKA, NORTH DAKOTA, OKLAHOMA, SOUTH DAKOTA, TEXAS, and WASHINGTON.

**Whig** a person who subscribes to a left-of-center political ideology.

**Whig Party** a political party, the precursor of the REPUBLICAN PARTY. It was the main alternative to the DEMOCRATIC PARTY before the CIVIL WAR.

**Whiskey Rebellion** an unsuccessful 1794 revolt by PENNSYLVANIA farmers against a tax on whiskey.

**Whiskey Ring** a scandal of ULYSSES S. GRANT's administration involving an attempt by a group of conspirators, led by Orville Babcock, the president's personal secretary, to divert liquor taxes to personal accounts.

**whistle-blower** a person who exposes or denounces an illegal or corrupt practice in a corporation or government agency by going over the heads of his superiors and informing the authorities.

**Whistler, James McNeill** 1834–1903. Painter. Whistler moved to England as a young man and established his reputation in the art circles of London and Paris. His most famous painting is *Whistler's Mother*, his 1872 portrait of his mother.

**white bread**  slang for a white person who is part of mainstream society.

**White, E. B.**  1899–1985. Writer. White set the standards of elegiac writing in *The New Yorker's* "Talk of the Town" column. He also wrote two classics for children: *Charlotte's Web* (1952) and *Stuart Little* (1945). With William Strunk, Jr., he wrote the classic *The Elements of Style* (1959), a handbook for writers.

**White English**  English as spoken by white Americans, as distinguished from BLACK ENGLISH.

**White House**  the executive residence of the president of the United States in WASHINGTON, D.C., originally built by James Hoban (1762–1831). The original design was completed in 1800.

**White Slave Traffic Act**  See MANN ACT.

**white slavery**  trafficking in white females for the purpose of prostitution.

**White, Stanford**  1853–1906. Architect. As partner in the McKim, Mead and White architectural firm, he was one of the most influential architects of the latter half of the 19th century. His masterpiece was MADISON SQUARE GARDEN in New York City, on whose rooftop he was shot to death by the jealous husband of one of his paramours.

**white trash**  a derogatory term for poor or improvident whites living in squalor, especially in the SOUTH.

**White, William Allen**  1868–1944. Journalist. Known as the Sage of Emporia, White was one of the best-read journalists of his day, known for his faithful portrayals of middle-class midwestern values.

**white-collar**  describing employees who work in office or professional settings, as opposed to industrial workers (see BLUE-COLLAR). They are so called because their nonphysical work rarely causes their clothing to become dirty; thus such workers can wear white shirts to work.

**white-shoe**  associated with the privileged and elite class in society.

**Whitman, Walt** 1819–1892. Poet. Whitman revolutionized poetry with his free verse and unconventional lifestyle. His *Leaves of Grass* is now considered one of the greatest poetic works of the 19th century.

**Whitney, Eli** 1765–1825. Inventor. Whitney is best known for inventing the COTTON GIN, which revolutionized the processing of raw cotton. He later manufactured firearms for the U.S. government.

**Whittier, John Greenleaf** 1807–1892. Quaker poet. He is remembered as the authentic voice of rural NEW ENGLAND.

**WI** WISCONSIN. (The official two-letter post office abbreviation.)

**widow's mandate** the tradition of appointing the widow of a dead governor, representative, or senator to complete the unexpired term of her husband.

**wild card** a sports team that qualifies for championship play-offs by winning an arbitrary play-off among second-place teams.

**Wild West** See OLD WEST.

**Wild West Show** a combination of a rodeo and a circus, founded in 1883 by BUFFALO BILL, which toured the United States and Europe until 1916. Among its featured participants were Annie Oakley (1860–1926), legendary for her marksmanship, and SITTING BULL.

**Wilder, Thornton Niven** 1897–1975. Novelist and playwright. Wilder won a PULITZER PRIZE for his novel *The Bridge of San Luis Rey* (1927), which dealt with the collapse of an ancient rope bridge in Peru in the 18th century. He went on to win two more Pulitzer Prizes, one for the enduring American drama *Our Town* (1938) and one for his comedic play *The Skin of Our Teeth* (1942).

**wildlifer** a person who advocates the protection of wildlife.

**Willard, Emma Hart** 1787–1870. Educator. A pioneer in women's education, Willard was the founder of the successful Troy Female Seminary. She also worked hard to train more women teachers and improve teaching techniques.

**Williams, (Hiram) Hank** 1923–1953. Singer. An original COUNTRY MUSIC star who blended GOSPEL MUSIC and black hillbilly music to establish himself as a pioneer in the genre.

**Williams, Roger** 1603–1683. Colonial leader. Founder of the Colony of RHODE ISLAND, Williams was one of the earliest proponents of the separation of church and state and of religious liberty.

**Williams, Tennessee** 1911–1983. Playwright. Williams's prolific output has been matched by few others. He wrote some of the most critically acclaimed plays in theater history: *The Glass Menagerie* (1945), *A Streetcar Named Desire* (1947), *Cat on a Hot Tin Roof* (1954), and *The Night of the Iguana* (1961). His plays dealt with dysfunctional families and lost and lonely souls, many of them modeled on members of his own family.

**Wilson, Edmund** 1895–1972. Critic and novelist. Wilson's erudition and flair for language made him a fearsome critic among the literary intelligentsia. Alternatively a serious scholar and a lively popularizer, Wilson's talents were far-ranging and covered biography, politics, history, religion, and social mores.

**Wilson, Woodrow** 1856–1924. Twenty-eighth president of the United States (1913–1921). His FOURTEEN POINTS listed the conditions for peace following WORLD WAR I.

**Windy City** Chicago, ILLINOIS, a city subject to gusts from LAKE MICHIGAN.

**Wisconsin** a state in the U.S. MIDWEST, known as the Badger State. Madison is its capital, and Milwaukee is its largest city. Its state bird is the robin, and its state flower is the wood violet. Abbreviated WI.

**Wise, Isaac Mayer** 1819–1900. Rabbi who was the chief architect of Reform Judaism. He was responsible for founding the Union of American Hebrew Congregations (1873), the Hebrew Union College (1875), and the Central Conference of American Rabbis (1889).

**witch hunt** the persecution of a person or group holding undesirable or unpopular opinions and beliefs.

***Wizard of Oz, The Wonderful*** a 1900 children's novel by L. Frank Baum (1856–1919), later made into a popular 1939 movie.

**Wobblies** members of the INDUSTRIAL WORKERS OF THE WORLD.

**Wolfe, Thomas** 1900–1938. Writer. Wolfe's literary reputation rests on a single masterpiece, *Look Homeward Angel* (1929), and on his productive relationship with Maxwell Perkins, editor at the publishing house of Scribner's.

**Wolverine State** MICHIGAN.

**Women's Christian Temperance Union** an organization founded in the 1870s to improve public morality by advocating abstinence from alcohol. Abbreviated WCTU.

**Wood, Grant** See AMERICAN GOTHIC.

**Woodhull, Victoria** 1838–1927. Pioneering feminist. Woodhull advocated free love, women's suffrage, and birth control. She ran as the presidential candidate of the Equal Rights Party in 1872, becoming the first woman to run for president in the United States.

**Woodstock** a ROCK AND ROLL music festival held near Woodstock, in the Catskills, NEW YORK in August 1969. Attended by nearly half a million young people, it marked the peak of the counterculture movement.

**Woollcott, Alexander** 1887–1943. Journalist and critic. Woollcott was a highly popular and influential drama critic for several New York newspapers in the 1920s. He was also a member of the famed literary group known as the ALGONQUIN ROUND TABLE.

**word processing** the use of computerized typesetting and editing to produce reports, letters, etc.

**workfare** a post-welfare program requiring welfare recipients to accept any work that is offered as a condition for further assistance.

**World Series** the final play-off marking the end of the annual BASEBALL season. Held every year since 1903 between the winners of the pennants of the AMERICAN LEAGUE and NATIONAL LEAGUE.

**World Trade Center** twin skyscrapers in lower MANHATTAN.

**World War I** a global war from 1914 to 1918 that began with the assassination of Archduke Francis Ferdinand of Austria-Hungary. The United States sided with the Allies (Britain, France, Russia, and Italy) against Germany, Austria, and the Ottoman Empire. Abbreviated WWI.

**World War II**  a global war from 1939 to 1945 that began with Hitler's invasion of Poland. The United States sided with the Allies (France, Britain, and the Soviet Union) against the Axis powers (Germany, Italy, and Japan). Abbreviated WWII.

**World Wide Web**  often, the Web. A global INTERNET network of graphics and information resources linked by HYPERTEXT. Abbreviated WWW.

**Wounded Knee**  a creek on the Pine Ridge SIOUX reservation in SOUTH DAKOTA, where a Sioux group led by Big Foot was massacred by U.S. government troops on December 29, 1890.

**WPA**  Works Progress Administration, a job-relief agency under the NEW DEAL, which sponsored a number of programs in construction and the arts.

**wrangler**  one who wrangles, or herds, cattle; a COWBOY.

**Wright Brothers**  Inventors and aviaton pioneers. Wilbur (1867–1912) and Orville (1871–1948) invented the first heavier-than-air self-propelled plane. Bicycle manufacturers by profession, the brothers built their successful biplane in 1903 and flew it at KITTY HAWK, NORTH CAROLINA.

**Wright, Frank Lloyd**  1867–1959. Architect. An important modern architect and a proponent of organic architecture designed to harmonize with and blend into the environment, Wright's presence still dominates architectural thinking. Among his works are the Imperial Hotel in Tokyo (1922), Fallingwater in Mill Run, PENNSYLVANIA (1937), and the Guggenheim Museum in New York City (1959). Wright designed more than 1,000 buildings, of which 400 were built and 280 are still standing.

**WV**  WEST VIRGINIA. (The official two-letter post office abbreviation.)

**WWI**  WORLD WAR I.

**WWII**  WORLD WAR II.

**WWW**  WORLD WIDE WEB.

**WY**  WYOMING. (The official two-letter post office abbreviation.)

**Wyeth, Andrew** 1917–. Painter. Wyeth, a popular landscapist, specialized in rural scenes and seascapes. His most famous painting is *Christina's World* (1948).

**Wyoming** a state in the western United States. Called the Equality State, its capital and largest city is Cheyenne. The meadowlark is the state bird, and the Indian paintbrush is the state flower. Abbreviated WY.

**WYSIWYG** what you see is what you get, a computer term guaranteeing that the hard copy will be the same as what appears on the screen.

# X

**Xer** a member of GENERATION X.

**XIT Ranch** a TEXAS cattle ranch in the late 19th century that covered roughly three million acres.

**Xmas** Christmas.

**X-rated** pornographic.

# Y

**Y, the** the YMCA or YWCA.

**Yale University** the third-oldest institution of higher learning in the United States, founded by Congregationalists in 1701 and named in honor of Elihu Yale, the British governor of Madras Province in India. It is located in New Haven, CONNECTICUT, and belongs to the IVY LEAGUE.

**Yankee** 1. originally a pejorative term for a NEW YORK Dutchman. Possibly from Jan Kees. 2. During the CIVIL WAR, any Northerner. 3. later applied to any New Englander. 4. in international usage, any American. Also, *Yank*.

**"Yankee Doodle"** a song that was popular with American soldiers during the REVOLUTIONARY WAR and remains a well-known patriotic song today.

**yard sale** the sale of old and used household or personal belongings, usually held in the front or backyard of a house.

**yellow brick road** the road to Oz in THE WONDERFUL WIZARD OF OZ.

**yellow pages** the classified section of a telephone book.

**yellow ribbon** an expression of solidarity with service personnel abroad or with a victim of a crime.

**yellowback** See DIME NOVEL.

**Yellowhammer State** ALABAMA.

235

**Yellowstone National Park**  a national park in WYOMING, MONTANA, and IDAHO that is surrounded by the ROCKY MOUNTAINS. Its features include OLD FAITHFUL, and many other geysers, petrified forests, and evergreen forests. Established in 1872, Yellowstone was the first national park in the United States.

**Yinglish**  blend of English and Yiddish; English marked by the extensive incorporation of Yiddish words and phrases.

**YMCA**  Young Men's Christian Association. Established in England in 1844, a network of nonprofit corporations that provide athletic, recreational, and educational services, as well as rooms to rent for transients, all at a minimal cost. Further abbreviated as the Y.

**YMHA**  Young Men's Hebrew Association. See JEWISH COMMUNITY CENTERS.

**Yosemite National Park**  a national park in CALIFORNIA containing the highest waterfalls in the continent.

**Young, Brigham**  1801–1877. Mormon leader. As successor to JOSEPH SMITH, Brigham Young led the exodus of MORMONS to UTAH, which he established as the stronghold of Mormon faith.

**Young Men's Hebrew Association**  See JEWISH COMMUNITY CENTERS.

**Young Women's Hebrew Association**  See JEWISH COMMUNITY CENTERS.

**yo-yo**  going up and down like a yo-yo, a toy spun up and down on a string.

**yuppie** AND **yuppy**  a young urban professional.

**YWCA**  Young Women's Christian Association. Founded in 1858, an organization providing athletic, recreational, and educational services to women at a minimal cost. Further abbreviated as the Y.

**YWHA**  Young Women's Hebrew Association. See JEWISH COMMUNITY CENTERS.

**zero population growth** a state of static population in which annual births are offset by an equal number of deaths.

**Ziegfeld, Florenz, Jr.** 1867–1932. Theatrical producer. Ziegfeld was an impresario who specialized in creating extravagant and ornate theatrical revues, especially ZIEGFELD'S FOLLIES.

***Ziegfeld's Follies*** a variety show organized by impresario FLORENZ ZIEGFELD that ran from 1907 to 1931. It featured a chorus line of Ziegfeld girls.

**zine** short form for magazine. Generally applied to alternative magazines with limited circulation catering to a select group.

**ZIP** See ZIP CODE.

**zip code** a five-digit postal routing code introduced by the U.S. Postal Service in 1963. Recently, a four-digit extension has been used in addition to the five-digit code, but its use has not yet been made mandatory. From ZIP, acronym for Zone Improvement Plan.

**Zuni** 1. a tribe of NATIVE AMERICANS who now live in NEW MEXICO. 2. a Native American pueblo in NEW MEXICO. 3. the language spoken by the ZUNI.

**zydeco** a black musical form dating to the 1950s that combines BLUES and Cajun styles.